Perspectives on
the Southeast

Perspectives on the Southeast

Linguistics, Archaeology, and Ethnohistory

Patricia B. Kwachka, Editor

Southern Anthropological Society Proceedings, No. 27
Mary W. Helms, Series Editor

The University of Georgia Press
Athens and London

Southern Anthropological Society

Founded 1966

Published by the University of Georgia Press
Athens, Georgia 30602
© 1994 by Southern Anthropological Society
All rights reserved

Set in 11 on 13 Times Roman
The paper in this book meets the guidelines for permanence and durability of the Committee on Production Guidelines for Book Longevity of the Council on Library Resources.

Printed in the United States of America
98 97 96 95 94 C 5 4 3 2 1
98 97 96 95 94 P 5 4 3 2 1

Library of Congress Cataloging in Publication Data
Perspectives on the Southeast : linguistics, archaeology, and ethnohistory /
    Patricia B. Kwachka, editor.
        p. cm.—(Southern Anthropological Society proceedings ; no. 27)
        Includes bibliographical references.
        ISBN 0-8203-1592-3 (alk. paper).—ISBN 0-8203-1593-1 (pbk. :
    alk. paper)
        1. Indians of North America—Southern States—Antiquities. 2. Indians
    of North America—Southern States—Languages. 3. Indians of North
    America—Southern States—Social conditions. 4. Ethnohistory—Southern
    States. 5. Ethnoarchaeology—Southern States. 6. Southern States—
    Antiquities. I. Kwachka, Patricia B. II. Series.
    GN2.S9243 no. 27
    [E78.S65]
    301 s—dc20
    [975'.01]   93-15728

British Library Cataloging in Publication Data available

Contents

Preface

The purpose of this volume is to facilitate cross-disciplinary conversations in the many fields focusing on questions regarding the distribution, organization, and relationships of southeastern Native American groups. The following essays were first presented as papers at the 1992 Southern Anthropological Society keynote symposium, "The Southeast at the Time of Columbus: Evidence from Linguistics and Archaeology."[1] Although their diversity precludes an overarching summary, these essays all point to two crucial issues currently affecting southeastern research. First, archaeological data are essential in the reconstruction of culture histories. Linguistics and ethnohistory may provide relative sequences or probable scenarios, but confirmation resides in the archaeological record. Conversely, the implications of an archaeological site may be absolute with respect to time but ambiguous with respect to ethnicity. Successful scholarship thus depends on the formation of intellectual confederacies, a difficult task in today's highly specialized academic environment. Second, until very recently all our evidence—whether archaeological, linguistic, or ethnohistoric—has been adventitious and sparse, depending on the vagaries of funding, the location of public works, or the serendipitous discovery of a text or a site. Given both the time depth and the sheer geography of the history we wish to understand, a critical mass of information adequate to a specific question at a specific place and time has been lacking. The past decade, however, has seen a flowering of interest in and research on southeastern questions. We are now at a juncture in the history of southeastern studies when the accumulation of information and perspectives allows us to reexamine previous conclusions, propose alternative interpretations, and ask new questions. This volume represents an effort in that direction.

The essays are arranged according to time and location. The first three address broad questions of southeastern interethnic relationships based on evidence from languages. Arguing on the basis of the distribution of linguistic traits, T. Dale Nicklas posits a protoassociation of Muskogean and Siouan. This initial association was followed by migrations and subsequent realignments that resulted in several overlapping linguistic "provinces" that share features not only across individual languages but across language families as well. The boundaries of these provinces both suggest the limits of social interaction and delineate spheres of cultural influence.

In examining patterns of loanword diffusion within the Muskogean languages, Jack Martin locates the dynamic nexus in Creek and implies, on the basis of a similar pattern for European loans, a relatively lengthy and stable network of internal and external social relationships. The pattern of diffusion suggests, moreover, that Mary Haas's 1941 classification of Muskogean language relationships is based on characteristics resulting from diffusion rather than from internal development and divergence.

As the Southeast evolved into the complex system of polities referred to as Mississippian, the density of communicative networks must have correspondingly increased. Emanuel J. Drechsel proposes that the necessary degree of intergroup communication could have been achieved only through a pidgin, Mobilian Jargon, and that this jargon therefore preceded contact.

Another concomitant of complex polities and increased interaction is hostility. Through a reanalysis of archaeological and ethnohistorical data, David H. Dye evaluates the role of warfare in the maintenance of chiefly polities and in their destabilization during the protohistoric period. He proposes that warfare not only procured surplus labor, prestige goods, and food but also legitimized and supported hierarchical social organization.

The social dislocations surrounding the decline of the Mississippian period confuse reconstructions of that time. Michael P. Hoffman reassesses available archaeological, linguistic, and ethnohistorical evidence to identify the ethnic affiliation of a group inhabiting eastern Arkansas during this period, positing a Tunica presence where Quapaw had previously been assumed.

A problem that the internal reconstruction of language relationships cannot address is the time at which various developments took place. Geoffrey Kimball attempts to overcome this by identifying items of Koasati material culture that are reconstructable in the prehistoric and protohistoric lexicon. He suggests that if these items can first be located in the archaeological record, it should then be possible to attach linguistic identities to assemblages of artifacts and, moreover, dates to linguistic groups.

To the south, in what is now central Mississippi, there is very little evidence of Mississippian cultures. By 1700, however, the area was occupied by the Choctaw. Kenneth H. Carleton examines ceramics for traces of the Choctaws' previous whereabouts and concludes, based on a mixture of elements, both structural and artistic, that the Choctaws associated with remnant groups before they came to central Mississippi.

In Spanish Florida of the sixteenth through the eighteenth centuries John H. Hann finds reflections of politically complex chiefdoms in patterns of nomenclature employed by missionaries and explorers to refer to local leaders. Charting the distribution of terms, he documents the wide participation of peoples from north Florida to North Carolina and Tennessee in hierarchical social organizations. At the same time, the absence of specific terms among several groups suggests their isolation from the mainstream.

Greg Keyes explores the degree to which contemporaneous social organization influences the interpretation of symbolic culture, pointing out that the descendants of chiefdoms, even though they may be linguistically and ethnically intact, adapt myths to fit their current social circumstances. To imbue persistent motifs with archaic interpretations is to portray societies as static.

Theda Perdue, following the course of southeastern social upheaval into the nineteenth century, proposes that the popularity of the Cherokee syllabary was due to its reinterpretation as a symbol of revitalization rather than of "civilization." Literacy represented knowledge, the defining characteristic of a responsible Cherokee.

Finally, John H. Moore brings us thoroughly into the twentieth century by reminding us of the persistence of cultural traits. Contemporary cultures may well maintain their predecessors' institutions, even their artifacts, reinterpreted according to current cosmologies. Extrapolation by analogy from current ethnography may therefore provide ethnographers and archaeologists alike with clues to ancestral cultures.

PATRICIA B. KWACHKA

NOTE

1. It is unfortunate that two excellent papers on Muskogean languages' affiliations (Pam Munro, "Gulf and Yuki-Gulf," and Aaron Broadwell, "Reconstructing Proto-Muskogean Language and Prehistory: Preliminary Results") were unable to be sufficiently condensed for inclusion in this volume.

Perspectives on
the Southeast

Linguistic Provinces of the
Southeast at the Time of Columbus

T. Dale Nicklas

The history of the Southeast to the time of Columbus can be reconstructed based on evidence from the fields of archaeology, ethnology, human genetics, or historical linguistics. Ultimately, any hypothesis will have to be consistent with the observations of all four fields. Hypotheses based on linguistic evidence alone can identify shifting patterns of contact between the peoples of the Southeast, at least those whose dialects survived to be documented. This is perhaps the principal contribution linguistics can make. But historical linguistics cannot locate language events absolutely in time and space; at best it can establish only relative chronologies and locations. Absolute determinations require collaboration with the other fields, archaeology in particular. An excellent example of this is Robert L. Rankin's paper "On Siouan Chronology" (1992), which suggests dates for events in Siouan based on the sharing of terms for cultural traits whose approximate dates of introduction are known through archaeological studies.

The question is, then, what are the linguistic provinces within the Southeast that might correlate with archaeological traditions? To answer this question we must select a list of traits and then compare them among all the languages in the Southeast. In addition, we must test the languages on the marches of the Southeast to determine the true boundaries of the border provinces.

This is the approach followed in this essay. The traits compared were selected by taking subsystems of grammar known to be covered in available works, or which could be analyzed relatively easily using available texts. The emphasis is therefore on phonology and morphology to the exclusion of syntax and vocabulary. Although this results in a fairly limited list of traits, the provinces described here developed easily, and their boundaries appeared sharply, which gives me reason to think that they may survive the inclusion of a wider range of traits. The extensions of traits westward from the lower Mississippi Valley and northward from Catawba have not yet been tested.

The linguistic provinces described below are simply smaller language areas in the greater language area of the Southeast, which is composed of languages that share traits as a result of borrowing rather than common inheritance or chance. The condition for borrowing is communication by way of a shared language, which means bilingualism in the case of borrowing across language boundaries. Factors that encourage communication and bilingualism include political union (including subjugation), trade relations, certain types of exogamy, fostering, and the adoption or enslavement of captives. In general, where genes are flowing and artifacts are diffusing, language traits are spreading. The desire to emulate is apparently a factor in determining the direction of borrowing.

There are two types of barriers to the spread of a trait: geographical and social. Mountains and dry regions seem to be more effective geographical barriers than woods and waters. In fact, navigable waters appear to join rather than separate peoples. Distance can be a geographical barrier. Social barriers are characterized by the absence of the social factors that encourage bilingualism or by the absence of the desire to emulate.

Events can create the impression of barriers where none existed. The classic case of this is a chain of languages, each linked to its neighbors on either side by shared traits, and the languages at the extremes sharing few or no traits. If the central language or languages are eliminated from the chain, as by emigration or extinction, this creates the appearance of a barrier between the languages left on either side. We are not yet in a position to discern where this happened in the Southeast, but there is reason to believe that many languages became extinct before they were ever documented (Speck 1907; Haas 1945, 1971; Crawford 1975).

When a trait is used to support a linguistic province, the assumption is that all the languages sharing that trait acquired it from one language, either directly or indirectly. There is occasionally a more or less equally viable hypothesis that the languages without the trait share the more recent innovation of discarding it. This should be kept constantly in mind.

From the foregoing, keeping in mind the provisional nature of this study, it seems likely that the conditions for bilingualism were stronger within the borders of these provinces than across them. We should therefore expect the provinces to correlate with archaeological traditions, gene frequency distributions, and culture areas.

I have significant firsthand knowledge of only Choctaw among the languages I compared. My information about all the other languages came from the grammars and sketches listed below. In most cases the material can be easily located in these sources, so I cite page numbers only when there is more than one treatment of a language, when the material is not easily locatable, or when a collateral source is used. In some cases the analysis is my own and differs from that of my sources.

The languages I dealt with and their principal sources are the following: Alabama (Lupardus 1982; Montler and Hardy 1990), Algonquian (Bloomfield 1946), Apalachee (Kimball 1987), Atakapa (Swanton 1929b; and ongoing analysis of Gatschet and Swanton 1932), Biloxi (ongoing analysis of Dorsey and Swanton 1912), Caddo (Chafe 1976:55–82), Catawba (Siebert 1945; Voorhis no date), Cherokee (Pulte 1975a), Chickasaw (Pulte 1975b; Munro 1987c), Chitimacha (Swadesh 1946a), Choctaw (Nicklas 1974, 1979a), Creek (Gatschet 1892), Dhegiha Siouan, including Quapaw (Boas 1906; Rankin 1975, 1977, 1987b, 1988b, 1988c), Hitchiti (Gatschet 1892), Iroquoian (Chafe 1967, 1970; Mithun 1979), Koasati (Kimball 1985), Proto-Muskogean (Booker 1980; Haas 1946b, 1969:52–58), Natchez (Haas 1979a; Swanton 1991), Timucua (Granberry 1990), Tunica (Haas 1946a), and Yuchi (Wagner 1934).

THE LOWER MISSISSIPPI VALLEY

The Lower Mississippi Valley core area encompasses Natchez, Tunica to the north, and Atakapa and Chitimacha to the south. This province, which appears to correspond to the Lower Valley archaeological tradition, is rather sharply distinguished from the Northern Tier to the north and Muskogean to the east. Some traits appear to extend eastward along the coasts, touching Biloxi, Timucua, and Catawba. Whether these traits extended to languages of the interior displaced by the Muskogean expansion cannot yet be determined. Significantly, languages contiguous to the Lower Mississippi Valley do not seem to have influenced it in recent times; that is, the desire to emulate was unidirectional.

Genetic relationships have been proposed for Natchez and Muskogean (Swanton 1924; Haas 1956); Tunica, Atakapa, and Chitimacha (Swanton 1919; Swadesh 1946b); and all of these combined under the term "Gulf" (Haas 1951, 1952). These Gulf languages may in turn be related to Algonquian (Haas 1958). These proposed genetic relationships do not account for the traits that bind the Lower Mississippi Valley as a province.

The following traits are characteristic of the Lower Valley core languages:

1. Resonants were devoiced before voicelessness in all four languages, with further transition to *h*, regularly in Chitimacha (Swadesh 1946b), sporadically in Natchez (Haas 1956).
2. A single pronominal series is used to mark alienable and inalienable possession.
3. The demonstrative precedes the noun. Only Siouan to the north and Choctaw-Chickasaw to the east have the opposite order.
4. Subject-object verb inflection rather than actor-patient inflection (but see item 15).
5. Subject prefixes precede object prefixes (except Chitimacha, where the situation does not arise).[1]
6. No inclusive first person.

THE COASTAL EXTENSION OF THE LOWER VALLEY

Lower Mississippi Valley traits appear to have spread along the Gulf and Atlantic coasts, with demonstrable effects on Biloxi, Timucua, and Catawba, the only documented coastal languages.

Biloxi forms a subgroup within Siouan with Ofo and Tutelo. The Biloxi were first encountered by Europeans on the Pascagoula River some miles inland (Dorsey and Swanton 1912), but subsequently they lived among the Tunica near Marksville, Louisiana (Haas 1968). Biloxi thus represents the migration of a Northern Tier language into the Gulf coastal plain. Several of its original Northern Tier traits have yielded to Lower Valley traits, giving evidence of a Lower Valley extension along the Gulf Coast. These include items 4, 5, and 6; that is, Siouan actor-patient verb inflection has been transformed into subject-object inflection, with the subject prefix before the object prefix, the Siouan order being patient before actor (first person before second person in some languages; see Nicklas 1991), and the category of inclusive person was eliminated by loss of the exclusive first person morphemes.

Julian Granberry (1987) asserts that Timucua is a South American immigrant. If he is correct, and he appears to be, the study of the typologies of the language in its homeland and along its route of migration should show whether correspondences between Timucua and the Lower Valley languages are accidental or the result of contact. Evidence of Lower Valley influence on Timucua includes items 2, 3, 4, 5, and 6. Except for item 4, these traits provide sharp contrast with the Muskogean languages that bordered Timucua on the north in historic times.

Timucua and Natchez share two additional traits, the second of which is so arbitrary and uncommon that it is difficult to avoid the conclusion that contact is the explanation:

7. The possessive affixes are suffixes.
8. If the possessor is plural, rather than use a plural possessive suffix, a circumlocution with the copula is preferred. One says, in effect, "he who is a father to us" for "our father" (Swanton 1991:72; Granberry 1990:82).

While Catawba is in some sense a Siouan language retaining many Siouan or Northern Tier traits, two traits appear to link it to Timucua and the Lower Mississippi Valley province, namely items 4 and 6. While only two, these traits contrast sharply with those of all the documented languages that bordered Catawba in historic times and therefore may well represent the most remote extension of the Lower Mississippi Valley.

It should be noted that in this chain, if a more remote language shares a trait with the Lower Valley, the intervening languages share the trait also. The exceptions—Biloxi's lack of items 2 and 3—are perhaps due to Biloxi's more recent contact with the Lower Valley compared with Timucua.

THE NORTHERN TIER

The Northern Tier province comprises Catawba and certain Siouan languages, Yuchi, and Cherokee and occupies a band running roughly from the mouth of the Ohio River eastward across Tennessee to the Carolinas, bordered on the north by Algonquian and Iroquoian, and on the south by the Lower Valley and Muskogean provinces. Cherokee represents an Iroquoian intrusion into the Northern Tier. It may be that Proto-Siouan itself belonged to this province.

Siouan languages in the Southeast fall into three subgroups: Catawba; Tutelo, Ofo, and Biloxi; and Dhegiha. The precise nature of the relationship between Catawba and the other Siouan languages has not been determined, so it is customary to speak of "Catawba and Siouan." Tutelo and Ofo are not included in this sample. The third subgroup, Dhegiha, includes Quapaw, Kansa-Osage, and Ponca-Omaha (Rankin 1988b).

There is some evidence of genetic relationships between Siouan and Yuchi, and Siouan, Caddoan, and Iroquoian (Chafe 1976). If these languages are in fact related, then all the Northern Tier languages are related. These distant relationships, however, do not explain the traits that bind the Northern Tier together in historic times.

The Northern Tier province is not as uniform as the Lower Mississippi Valley, a reflection of the facts that Dhegiha Siouan and Yuchi also belong to the younger Northeast Corner province, that Catawba also belongs to the Coastal Extension of the Lower Valley, and that Cherokee is intrusive and shows recent influence from the Muskogean languages to the south.

While there are clear connections between Northern Tier languages and others in the Southeast, there are also connections to the north with Algonquian and Iroquoian, stronger in the latter case.

Implied by the foregoing, the Northern Tier contrasts with the Lower Valley in the following respects: (a) there is no devoicing of resonants; (b) different pronominal series are used to mark alienable and inalienable possession; (c) in Siouan and Catawba, the closest neighbors to the Lower Valley, the demonstrative follows the noun, while it precedes it in Yuchi and Cherokee; (d) there is actor-patient verb inflection rather than subject-object inflection (except Catawba); (e) object/patient verb prefixes precede subject/actor prefixes (except in Cherokee, which continues the Iroquoian pattern, and some Siouan languages, including Dhegiha, which have first person before second person); (f) the inclusive first person is universal (except in Catawba). Algonquian is in accord with a and f, and the demonstrative precedes the noun. Iroquoian is in accord with a, b, d, and f. Proto-Muskogean conforms to all these Northern Tier patterns, except the original order of the demonstrative has not been determined (see below).

Additional traits that bind the Northern Tier together include the following:

9. Rectangular oral vowel inventories; that is, there are equal numbers of front and back vowels, counting *a* as a back vowel, in Proto-Algonquian, Proto-Iroquoian (but not Cherokee), Catawba, Yuchi, and Dhegiha Siouan (but not Proto-Siouan or Siouan generally; see Rankin 1975). More to the point, one would like to know whether *a* is bright or dark in each language, but this kind of phonetic detail is not available.
10. Ancient nasal vowels. Includes Iroquoian but not Algonquian.
11. Voiced stop series in Catawba, Yuchi, and Cherokee, perhaps due to the southeastern lenition (item 32), reflect an earlier contrast between fortis and lenis stops.
12. Contrastive fortis (aspirated) stop series. In Cherokee and Catawba these currently contrast with voiced stops rather than voiceless lenis stops.
13. The inalienable possessive prefix is identical with the actor/subject prefix in Iroquoian, Cherokee, Catawba, Yuchi, and Biloxi. In Siouan generally and in Muskogean it is identical with the patient/object prefix.

THE NORTHWEST CORNER

The Northwest Corner province consists of Yuchi, Dhegiha Siouan (particularly Quapaw), and Tunica. This province is younger than the Northern Tier and the Lower Mississippi Valley, which it overlaps. This relative youth is indicated by the fact that, with one exception, it includes Dhegiha rather than Siouan as a whole. There is other evidence that it is a relatively recent association.

Five traits characterize this province, although not all are universal within it:

14. Lack of vowel length in Tunica and Quapaw; Yuchi authorities are in conflict. Possibly an adaptation in the case of Quapaw to an older Tunica pattern.
15. Tunica has transformed its Lower Valley subject-object inflection into the actor-patient type found in Siouan and Yuchi.
16. Inflectional suffixed auxiliaries, consisting of verbs of location ("to be there"), mark priority in time in Tunica and Yuchi.
17. Inanimate as well as animate nouns are marked for gender and number in Tunica, Yuchi, and Quapaw by a cluster of traits reminiscent of Algonquian. The Tunica and Yuchi systems are quite similar. All other Southeastern languages mark the plural of human nouns only (with a few exceptions) except Timucua, which, however, has a distinct marking system.
18. In Siouan and Yuchi dative verbal prefixes agree with the "person to whom" or the possessor of the direct object. The beneficiary is marked by the "second dative" (Boas and Deloria 1939:86) prefixes, consisting of a dative prefix agreeing with the person of the beneficiary, incremented by a following non-anaphoric third person form of the dative.

MUSKOGEAN

The Muskogean languages do not fall into distinct subgroups. Chickasaw is one of a number of Choctaw dialects.[2] Seminole is one of a number of Creek dialects. Miccosukee is one of a number of Hitchiti dialects. Alabama and Koasati are said not to be mutually intelligible. If this is so, it appears to be the result of vocabulary replacement, as the phonological and grammatical differences between them appear to be no greater than what one finds among Choctaw dialects.

The geographic distribution of Muskogean languages suggests that the Muskogean family expanded to its historical boundaries relatively recently, which implies that it displaced other languages. Consistent with this is the fact that evidence of contact between Muskogean and other languages appears at roughly two levels. The first consists of traits that are more characteristic of Proto-Muskogean than the modern languages. These traits imply a connection with what became the Northwest Corner, suggesting a former Proto-Muskogean homeland in the middle Mississippi region.

The second consists of traits adopted during the divergence of the Muskogean dialectics. The entire Muskogean area has the appearance of a former continuous dialect area, with isoglosses running in several directions, which has been broken up into discrete languages by the loss of intermediate dialects. It has been argued that there are two extreme dialectic types, Choctaw to the west and Creek to the east, with the other languages in the middle being influenced now from the east, now from the west (Speck 1907; Haas 1979b). It does appear that these two extremes are the most innovative, and that their innovations are, to some extent, simplifications of the type one might expect from the absorption of other peoples. Alabama and Koasati have remained more conservative, suggesting that they occupied exclusive territories at a time when Choctaw and Creek were expanding into occupied territories or otherwise absorbing other peoples. Nevertheless, it is often convenient to refer to the eastern languages (Alabama, Koasati, Creek-Seminole, Hitchiti-Miccosukee, and Apalachee) as a group.

These impressions are consistent with an original Muskogean homeland in middle Mississippi, removal eastward to a new homeland in the region of eastern Mississippi and western Alabama, and subsequent expansion of Choctaw to the west and south, and of Creek, Hitchiti, and Apalachee to the east and south.

PROTO-MUSKOGEAN AREAL AFFINITIES

Some accord between Muskogean and Northern Tier traits has already been noted. The following traits link Proto-Muskogean with Siouan and Yuchi in particular:

19. Lexical and derivational suffixed auxiliaries are found in Proto-Muskogean and Proto-Siouan, also Natchez, and possibly formerly in Catawba.
20. The alienable possessive pronominal consists of the inalienable prefix plus an increment in Proto-Muskogean, Proto-Siouan, Catawba, and Pre-Natchez. The Muskogean series is then identical with its indirect object series, as is the case in Yuchi and Natchez.
21. Proto-Muskogean, Proto-Siouan, and Caddo all developed an inclusive first person based in part on indefinite third person

elements (Booker 1980; Chafe 1976; Nicklas 1979b; Robert L. Rankin, personal communication). The inclusive first person is also found in Proto-Algonquian, Proto-Iroquoian, and Yuchi.

22. Proto-Muskogean shares both the semantic and the formal distinctions between the dative and benefactive verbal prefixes found in Siouan and Yuchi (item 18).[3]

CHOCTAW-CHICKASAW AREAL AFFINITIES

Choctaw has two traits that suggest later influence from the Lower Mississippi Valley:

23. The fricative *s* became retroflex, then subsequently switched from apical to blade articulation, while the affricate *ts* continued apical articulation. The same changes appear to have occurred in Natchez and Atakapa. Pre-Choctaw *ts* subsequently became *s*.

24. The accommodation noted in item 25 below was accompanied by a change in the order of prefixes to actor-patient.

The following are noteworthy examples of later Northern Tier influence on Choctaw and Chickasaw:

25. Actor prefixes rather than suffixes. This brings Choctaw into line with the Northern Tier from Cherokee westward. To achieve this result, Choctaw generalized the minority class of Proto-Muskogean verbs with prefixes, at the expense of the much larger verb classes with infixes and suffixes (Haas 1969).

26. Choctaw dialects except Chickasaw have nasal vowels arising from regular loss of following preconsonantal *n* and *m*.

27. Chickasaw has developed a preconsonantal glottal stop from vowel length (Pulte 1975b). Dhegiha, Biloxi, possibly Siouan generally, and Shawnee also developed preconsonantal glottal stops, but from other sources (Rankin 1987b; Miller 1959).

28. The Choctaw demonstrative follows the noun, as in Catawba and Siouan. All other languages in the Southeast prefer the opposite order.

EASTERN MUSKOGEAN AREAL AFFINITIES

Innovations that distinguish Eastern Muskogean languages are seen in other languages found east of Yuchi and Choctaw. Koasati and Alabama do not share in these traits to the extent that Creek and Hitchiti do. The following appear to be significant:

29. The southeastern lenition (loss of aspiration and voicing between vowels) affected Creek and Hitchiti obstruants, and possibly Catawba, Cherokee, and Yuchi stops (item 11). This may be a southern extension of a more widespread phenomenon.

30. Actor/subject suffixes rather than prefixes predominate (Alabama, Koasati, Catawba) or are exclusive (Creek, Hitchiti, Apalachee; see Haas 1969; Kimball 1987).

MESO-AMERICAN INFLUENCES

One would expect to find linguistic traits linking the Southeast, especially the lower Mississippi Valley, with Meso-America, as archaeological traits do. A comparison of my list of southeastern provincial traits with traits common to Meso-America (Campbell et al. 1986), but not immediately beyond it, confirms this expectation.

Lyle Campbell, Terrence Kaufman, and Thomas Smith-Stark (1986) do not always describe the phonological traits they treat in sufficient detail to make firm comparisons. With that caveat, the following show possible Meso-American influence in the Southeast, or vice versa:

31. Devoicing of resonants is found in Meso-America and the Lower Valley (item 1).

32. Vowel harmony is a trait of several Meso-American languages, with details that vary from language to language. Vowel harmony is a prominent trait of Natchez in the Southeast and is known in Muskogean.

33. Retroflex sibilants are found in Meso-America and Natchez, whence they diffused northward to Tunica and Quapaw and eastward to Eastern Muskogean (Rankin 1978, 1988b), Choctaw (item 23), and possibly Timucua.

Campbell, Kaufman, and Smith-Stark (1986:553) list fifty-five calques common in Meso-America. The following, retaining the numbers they carry in the source, are found in Choctaw unless another language is cited; several are widespread in the Southeast, but no systematic search has been made for them. When there are two equivalents to the right of the equals sign, the rightmost is the Choctaw equivalent. It should be noted that in Muskogean *child* doubles as the diminutive suffix, so *hand child* would normally be interpreted as 'little hand', and so forth. The following calques are notable: (1) door = house mouth (Atakapa, Chitimacha); (2) bark = skin of tree, tree skin; (8) finger = child of hand, hand child; (23) to kiss = to suck; (24) to smoke = to suck; (31) vein = road of blood, blood road; (35) thumb = mother of hand, hand mother; (36) mano = child of metate (in Choctaw, pestle = mortar child); (48) alive = awake; (52) need = want, be wanted; (53) enter = house-enter (Natchez); (55) feather = fur.

Of these calques, 31, 35, and 48 coincide with the borders of the Meso-American language area; the others are widespread among some of the languages of that area, but not among those immediately adjacent to it.

NOTES

I gratefully acknowledge the encouragement and assistance of Karen M. Booker, Robert L. Rankin, and Paul Voorhis, who furnished materials not otherwise available to me and provided many helpful comments and insights. Heather K. Hardy and Janine Scancarelli added very helpful comments and suggestions. The errors, defects, and malinterpretations that are doubtless present are, however, mine. Unfortunately, space is insufficient for presenting details, including exceptions to the generalizations formulated here, or for marshaling the evidence supporting the claims I present here; that will have to appear elsewhere.

1. The order of subject/actor and object/patient affixes is based on the relative order of first and second person affixes only, where both are prefixes or both are suffixes. The third person is unmarked in some languages; where it is marked, it frequently appears farther from the stem than the first and second persons, sometimes as a clitic, suggesting that it is a recent innovation.

2. It is often erroneously stated in the literature that there are three dialects of Choctaw proper: Oklahoma Choctaw, Mississippi Choctaw, and Mississippi

Choctaw of Oklahoma. In fact, there appear to be three focal dialects and several intermediate forms. All three focal dialects are, however, found in both Oklahoma and Mississippi. For that matter, Choctaw dialects in Louisiana are also represented in Oklahoma and Mississippi. I have seen no evidence that Mississippi Choctaw of Oklahoma is anything other than a Choctaw dialect influenced somewhat by Chickasaw after removal to Oklahoma.

  3. I describe the "second dative" in Choctaw under "free dative" (Nicklas 1974:36). Charles Ulrich (1986:259–60) has questioned this analysis, but it is undoubtedly correct, synchronically for speakers I am familiar with as well as historically. Ulrich's informant may have restructured it. For the cognate construction in eastern Muskogean (Koasati), see Kimball (1985:123).

Modeling Language Contact in the Prehistory of the Southeastern United States

Jack Martin

Like elements of material culture, words can spread between populations. The study of the spread of these loanwords can provide information regarding directions and paths of contact, the types of items
traded, and something about the political relationships among speech
communities. I confine my attention here to the southeastern United
States and to the spread of indigenous and European loanwords. I will
show that both types of borrowing can be described by positing separate eastern and western spheres of influence, the former centering
on Creek-speaking populations, and the latter centering on Choctaw-
and Chickasaw-speaking populations. I then discuss the implications
such a model might have for internal groupings within the Muskogean
languages.

INDIGENOUS PATHS OF DIFFUSION

A number of loanwords occur in native languages of the Southeast.[1]
These are discussed below.

Modern speakers of Creek (Muskogean) use the word *tokná:wa*
'money, dollar'. Alabama and Koasati (also Muskogean) have a similar
form (*tokna:wa*). In Creek (but not in Alabama or Koasati), the word is
analyzable as *cató* 'rock, iron' and *koná:wa* 'bead', with a longer variant (*catokná:wa*) appearing in older sources. These facts suggest that
Alabama and Koasati borrowed the word from Creek.

A speaker of Alabama remembers a word *taklosa* 'black person'. Chickasaw and Choctaw (Muskogean) have similar forms *taklosa?* and *taklósa*, respectively. The word is not analyzable in Alabama; in Chickasaw and Choctaw the word appears to derive from *hattak* 'person' and *losa* 'black'. Alabama thus appears to have borrowed this word from Chickasaw or Choctaw.

Creek has a word *kolapâ:kin* 'seven', derived from *hokkol-* 'two' and *apâ:kin* 'added on' (Haas 1969:81). Cherokee (Iroquoian) borrowed this word (a special number in Cherokee culture) as *kahlkwo:ki*. The Cherokee word differs from words found elsewhere in Iroquoian, so the direction of borrowing is certain (Lounsbury 1961; Haas 1961, 1969:81).

Creek has a word *hóyₜiko:* 'oyster' (literally, 'doesn't stand'). Miccosukee (Muskogean) has a similar form *hôyₜiki.*[2] The direction of borrowing was probably from Creek to Miccosukee.[3] Three points provide the evidence for this directionality: (1) the word is analyzable in Creek but not in Miccosukee; (2) the Creek accent is characteristic of negatives, and this is presumably the source of the irregular accent pattern in Miccosukee; and (3) the difference in the quality of the final vowel is accounted for if the direction of borrowing was from Creek into Miccosukee (since Miccosukee neutralizes all noun-final vowels as /i/).

Creek has a noun *yatí:ka* 'interpreter' formed from the verb *yati:k-* 'interpret'. The noun was borrowed into Timucua as *yatiki* (Ballard 1982) and into Koasati as *iyatí:ka* (Geoffrey Kimball, personal communication). The Yuchi form *yatik?e* (Ballard 1982) was probably borrowed from Creek or Koasati. Since Creek and Yuchi are still in close contact, it is difficult to determine whether this is an early or recent loan.

Fox (Algonquian) *pine:wa* 'turkey' (or perhaps a similar form in some other Algonquian language) was borrowed into Creek as *pínwa* (Michelson 1935; Haas 1958). The Creek word has no obvious cognates within Muskogean.

Mary Haas (1958) identifies Choctaw *niŠkin* 'eye' (cf. Chickasaw *iŠkin*) as a possible loan from an Algonquian language. This form is reconstructable in Proto-Algonquian as *-Ški•nŠekwi* 'eye', *neŠki•nŠekwi* 'my eye' (Bloomfield 1946); there are no obvious cognates elsewhere in Muskogean.

Haas (c. 1940) suggests that a Shawnee (Algonquian) word for 'nut'

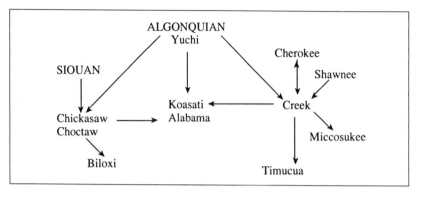

Fig. 1. Spread of indigenous words/affixes in the Southeast.

was borrowed into Creek as *paká:na* 'peach' (see also English *pecan,* also from an Algonquian language). The Creek word does not resemble any word in the other Muskogean languages.

Haas (c. 1940) suggests Cherokee *su:li* 'buzzard' is the source of Creek *solí.*

Geoffrey Kimball (1990) notes that a prefix *hi-* is added to numbers in some of the Siouan languages of the Southeast as well as in Chickasaw, Choctaw, and Alabama. Since this prefix is not found elsewhere in Muskogean, the direction of borrowing is presumably from Siouan into Muskogean.

Kimball (1991:473) suggests Yuchi *tsʔʌtha* 'turtle' is the source of Koasati *sattá* (and Alabama *satta*). Nothing similar appears in the other Muskogean languages.

Haas (1969:81) suggests that Biloxi (Siouan) /čuwahna/ 'cedar' is from a Muskogean language (from Choctaw, Alabama, Koasati *cowahla,* or from Chickasaw *cowāhlaʔ*). As Haas notes, Biloxi lacks /l/, so the replacement of /l/ with /n/ in this form is natural if Biloxi borrowed from Muskogean.

The arrows in Figure 1 reflect social relations—paths along which words diffused. The historical pattern that emerges is one in which words passed into Creek from the north and east (either directly or through intermediate languages), and words spread south and west from Creek into neighboring languages.

THE SPREAD OF EUROPEAN LOANWORDS

When European words spread between indigenous languages, they apparently followed the same paths followed by indigenous loanwords.[4] Most early Spanish loanwords, for example, were probably introduced through contact with Franciscan missions established among the Timucua, Guale, and Apalachee between 1565 and 1710 (Hudson 1976). These words spread to speakers of Creek and Hitchiti/Miccosukee, then to speakers of Koasati and Alabama, and finally to speakers of Chickasaw and Choctaw. Nine words support this pattern.

Spanish *frasco* 'flask' yields Creek *falá:sko* 'bottle' and Miccosukee *fala:ski* 'bottle'.

Spanish *capa* 'cape' yields Creek *ká:pa* 'coat' and Miccosukee *ka:pi* 'coat'.

Spanish *jarro* 'jar' yields Creek *há:lo* 'cup' and Miccosukee *hâ:li* 'cup'.

Spanish *soldado* 'soldier' yields Creek *solitá:wa*, Miccosukee *solita:wi*, Koasati *solita:wa*, and Apalachee *soldadoh*.

Spanish *tocino* 'bacon' yields Creek *tosí:na*, Miccosukee *tosi:ni*, and Alabama and Koasati *tosi:na*.

Spanish *chivato* 'goat' yields Creek *cowá:ta*, Miccosukee *cowa:ti*, and Alabama and Koasati *cowa:ta*.

Spanish *naranja* 'orange' yields Creek *yalá:ha*, Miccosukee *yala:hi*, Alabama *yala:ha*, and Koasati *yalaha*.

Spanish *vaca* 'cow' yields Creek *wá:ka*, Miccosukee *wa:ki*, Alabama and Koasati *wa:ka*, Choctaw *wa:k*, and Chickasaw *wa:kaʔ*.

Spanish *arroz* 'rice' yields Creek *aló:so*, Miccosukee *alo:si*, Alabama *o:nosi*, Koasati *alo:so*, Choctaw *onoš*, and Chickasaw *ha:lõ̌ši?*.

Note that Spanish loanwords in Alabama and Koasati form a subset of those in Creek and Miccosukee, and those found in Chickasaw and Choctaw are also found in the other languages.[5] This three-tiered pattern can be explained if we modify the model shown in Figure 1 slightly to allow two-way trade between Chickasaw and Alabama. The section of Figure 1 relevant to Spanish loanwords appears in Figure 2.

The spread of French loanwords is less extensive and less revealing. Units of money spread to Koasati, Alabama, and Choctaw.[6]

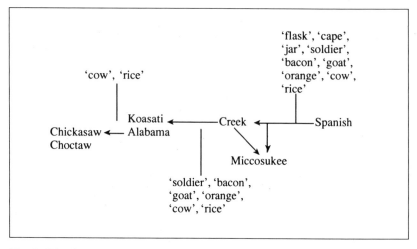

Fig. 2. Distribution of Spanish loanwords in Muskogean languages.

French *picaillon* 'small coin' yields Alabama, Koasati *pikayo* 'nickel', and Choctaw *pikayo* 'nickel'.

French *escalin* yields Alabama *(i)skali* 'bit, money', Koasati *skali* 'bit, money', and Choctaw *(i)skali* 'money'.

These data are consistent with the model in Figure 1.

IMPLICATIONS FOR "GENETIC" GROUPINGS
WITHIN MUSKOGEAN

It is sometimes difficult to determine whether similarities between languages are due to common descent or to diffusion. The difficulties in this area are evident in debates surrounding the internal classification of the Muskogean languages. Haas (1941) hypothesizes that Proto-Muskogean (PM) divided into Western Muskogean and Eastern Muskogean, as outlined in Figure 3. There are three main phonological correspondences supporting Haas's classification.

Western Muskogean *n* corresponds in some instances to Eastern *¢* (Haas 1941): Choctaw *tana* 'weave', Chickasaw *tanni*, Alabama and Koasati *ta¢a*, Hitchiti *ta¢-*, and Creek *ta¢-íta*.

Western *s* corresponds in some instances to Eastern *c* (Haas 1941):[7] Choctaw and Chickasaw *nosi* 'sleep', Alabama and Koasati *noci*, Hitchiti and Miccosukee *no:c-i:ki*, and Creek *noc-íta*.

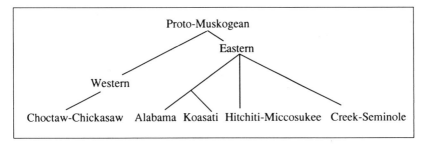

Fig. 3. Muskogean genetic classification (after Haas 1941).

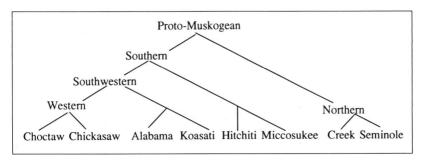

Fig. 4. Muskogean genetic classification (after Munro 1987b).

Final * . . . *ixo* yields . . . *i (h)* in Western Muskogean nouns and . . . *o* in Eastern nouns:[8] Choctaw *konih* 'skunk', Chickasaw *koni*, Alabama and Koasati *kono*, and Creek *konó*.

Pamela Munro (1985b, 1987a, 1987b) presents evidence for a different classification, one more similar to John Swanton's 1922 proposal (see Figure 4). The primary arguments for this classification are discussed below.

k^w developed in some environments into *b* in the southern languages and *k* in Creek (Haas 1947).

A 'passive' infix *-l-* occurs in the southern languages, possibly deriving from the PM reflexive prefix *ili-* (Munro 1987a, personal communication).

The southern languages have an unusual rule indicating plurals in verbs through deletion of a portion of the root (Broadwell, in press).

The southwestern languages have an unusual rule of assimilation affecting the *-li* auxiliary suffix (Munro 1985b).

The southwestern languages have an aspectual rule of grade formation indicated through gemination (Munro 1987a).

The southwestern languages may have spread the use of initial *a* in certain forms of objective person markers (Munro 1987b).

The southwestern languages show reflexes of plural **ha-* before certain first and second person person markers (Munro 1987a).

In the preceding sections I attempted to map paths of diffusion by examining clear examples of borrowing. The model in Figures 2 and 3 allows us to reexamine Haas's and Munro's classifications in this light. Consider, for example, Haas's (1941) *n:¢* correspondence. To account for these sets, Haas reconstructed an additional PM phoneme (**N*), which merged with **n* in Choctaw and Chickasaw and with **¢* in the Eastern Muskogean languages. The weakness of this approach is noted by Munro (1987a:3), who suggests that *n* may be an innovation within the Western Muskogean languages, Choctaw and Chickasaw.

The model in Figure 2 points to a possible source for this innovation. I argued above that the Western Muskogean languages were in contact with Siouan languages. This offers the possibility that Western Muskogean *n* and *s* might be the result of Siouan contact. Support for such a proposal would come from proof that the Siouan languages adjacent to Choctaw and Chickasaw had rules affecting the pronunciation of laterals and sibilants, rules that might have spread (incompletely) to Western Muskogean.

Speakers of Biloxi (Siouan) seem to have converted laterals into nasals when borrowing a word with a lateral from another language. As noted by Haas (1969:81, also discussed above), Biloxi speakers borrowed a word for 'cedar' from a Muskogean language (Choctaw, Alabama, and Koasati *cowahla*, or Chickasaw *cowãhlaʔ*). In so doing, they converted *l* to *n,* yielding Biloxi /čuwahna/. Another example of this sort (pointed out to me by Dale Nicklas) is Biloxi *tckanĕ́* 'nine', from Choctaw *cákkâ:li*. These examples establish a possible source within Siouan for Western Muskogean lateral-to-nasal shifts.

There are additional lateral/nasal correspondences that cannot be attributed to **N*. In some instances, Eastern *l* corresponds to Western *n* (or a nasalized vowel adjacent to *l*):

Creek *afallá:* 'poison ivy' versus Chickasaw *fannik* 'stinging
    plant'
Creek *lácci* 'branch' versus Choctaw, Chickasaw *naksiçs*

Alabama and Koasati *takkola* 'peach' versus Choctaw *takkon,* Chickasaw *takōlo*
Creek *aló:so* 'rice', Miccosukee *alo:si,* and Koasati *alo:so* versus Choctaw *onoŠ,* Chickasaw *ha:lōŠiʔ, haloŠiʔ* (see also Alabama *o:nosi*)

In other instances, Eastern *n* corresponds to Western *l* (sometimes accompanied by a nasalized vowel):

Alabama *wino:li* 'shake' and Koasati *winohli* versus Chickasaw *wilo:li*
Creek *tini:p-itá* 'smooth' and Hitchiti *tinibi* 'smooth' versus Choctaw *tilikpi* 'dull' and Chickasaw *tilikpi* 'round'
Hitchiti *honoli* 'bullfrog' and Alabama and Koasati *hanono* versus Choctaw *halōlabi* and Chickasaw *hali:lawiʔ*
Creek *ciȼókco* 'chipmunk' versus Choctaw *cinisa* and Chickasaw *cilīsaʔ*
Alabama *hana:biya* 'lizard' and Koasati (with metathesis) *hayabina* versus Choctaw *halābiya* 'skink' and Chickasaw *halamboʔ*
Koasati *bacano* 'hail' versus Chickasaw *bacaloŠa* 'sleet'
Koasati *kono:bi* 'throat' versus Choctaw *kolōbiŠ* (cf. Chickasaw *inōʔkopoloʔ*)

These sets (which are unexpected on Haas's account) point to variation in the pronunciation of laterals and nasals within Western Muskogean, a phenomenon reminiscent of Siouan lateral-to-nasal shifts of the type observed in Biloxi.

Variation in the pronunciation of sibilants is also found in Siouan (Rankin 1987a, 1988b). If the *s:c* correspondence can also be attributed to Siouan influence, two arguments for Haas's (1941) "genetic" classification could be reduced to known patterns of contact.

There is more specific evidence of Siouan influence on Choctaw and Chickasaw. Within Muskogean, falling tone in Alabama corresponds to glottal stop in Chickasaw and to a long vowel in Choctaw:

Alabama	Chickasaw	Choctaw	English
cinô:li	*cinoʔli*	*cono:li*	'pinch' (plural)
tóccî:na	*tócciʔna*	*tócci:na*	'three'[9]
táȼȼâ:pi	*táȼȼaʔpi*	*táȼȼa:pi*	'five'

Ulrich (in press) argues that Choctaw long vowels in forms like these derive from a sequence of vowel and glottal stop; the Chickasaw forms above are thus conservative. Additional evidence suggests that nonfinal glottal stops develop from falling tone:

$$\ldots\, C\hat{V}{:}CV > \ldots\, CV\text{?}CV > \ldots\, CV{:}CV$$

These developments have a synchronic reflex: in some Chickasaw verb forms (known as grades), either glottal stop or falling tone occurs depending on the shape of the verb (Munro 1985a). One interpretation of these data is that falling tone is realized synchronically as glottal stop, except where the syllable structure of the language blocks an additional consonant. It seems unlikely that glottal stop developed into falling tone; the latter is found in all branches of Muskogean, while glottal stop is more restricted.

Robert Rankin (1988b, 1988c) notes similar examples in Siouan and suggests an areal phenomenon. In Ponca, Biloxi, and Hidatsa, glottal stop was inserted postaccentually. The rule he reconstructs for Siouan is as follows:

$$(C)VCV'CV\text{-} > (C)VhC\hat{V}{:}CV\text{-} > (C)VhCV\text{?}CV\text{-}$$

On this analysis, a stressed syllable was preaspirated, with aspiration leading falling tone on the stressed syllable; falling tone subsequently led to glottalization (perhaps via creaky voice). The shift from falling tone to glottalization is identical with the development sketched above for Choctaw and Chickasaw. Attributing the Western Muskogean development here to spread of the Siouan rule reconstructed by Rankin would explain why glottal stop in this position is limited to a subset of the Muskogean languages. The direction of borrowing was apparently from Siouan to Muskogean, since Ponca and Hidatsa are more distant and show a similar phenomenon within Siouan.

Such a rule provides further support for the model in Figure 1.[10] In addition, it shows that phonological rules found in Siouan (specifically, lateral-to-nasal shifts and variation in the pronunciation of sibilants) could have influenced Western Muskogean.

Nicklas (this volume) suggests that the notion of the family tree fails to account for the complexity of relations in Muskogean (though he seems to accept such a model for Siouan and Caddoan). I have argued here that the apparent conflict between Haas's and Munro's classifications can be reduced to a traditional genetic classification (Munro's) combined with a fairly simple model of language contact (established independently by examining the spread of indigenous and European loanwords). It seems likely that the adequacy of the family tree as a model of linguistic classification ultimately depends on the origins of those divisions within communities contributing to diversification: in the Southeast, migration between rivers may have created sharp rifts in language contact, leading to clean splits in the data. It remains to be seen whether the patterns of diffusion established here can be linked to historical and archaeological data concerning contact in the Southeast.

NOTES

I am grateful to Pam Munro, Heather Hardy, and Aaron Broadwell for numerous discussions relating to the points addressed in this essay, and to Geoff Kimball, Dale Nicklas, Janine Scancarelli, and Emanuel Drechsel for useful comments. All mistakes are my own.

1. Previous studies discussing loanwords in the Southeast include Gatschet (1884), Sturtevant (1962), Ballard (1982), and Kimball (1991:473–76, this volume), among others. I have excluded proper names (which frequently have a more complex history) and loanwords in which the direction of borrowing is uncertain. The data cited in this paper are primarily from Munro et al. (1990), which itself draws on data from Haas and other primary sources. In transcribing the Muskogean languages, I use a colon after a vowel to represent a long vowel; ɬ is a voiceless lateral fricative; $\check{S}$ is as in English ca*sh;* c is usually as in English ca*tch;* ? is a glottal stop.

2. Miccosukee is often spelled Mikasuki in the scientific literature; my spelling conforms to that used by the Miccosukee Tribe of Florida.

3. The Creek word was apparently also borrowed into Koasati. Kimball (personal communication) cites a Koasati word *hohiʔʔikó* 'shellfish' from Haas's unpublished Koasati vocabulary. The vowel breaking and gemination in the Koasati form evidently reflect the effects of accent in Creek.

4. I ignore loanwords from English here, since English loans may reflect recent, parallel loans. One early loan from English, however, is Creek *wacína* 'Anglo-American' (from *Virginia*), apparently yielding Koasati *waciná* 'English' (Kimball 1991:474).

5. The spread of Spanish *trigo* 'wheat', *capitán* 'captain', and *azúcar* 'sugar' is slightly more complex: derivatives of Spanish *trigo* are found in all the languages except Miccosukee (where our data may be incomplete); words related to the Spanish *capitán* have been found in all but Choctaw and Alabama;

Spanish *azúcar* was borrowed into Creek and Miccosukee but also occurs unexpectedly in Chickasaw. Florida Seminole has a number of more recent Spanish loans not found in Creek or Oklahoma Seminole; e.g., *wilantaló* 'banana' (Spanish *plátano*), *alí:na* 'flour' (Spanish *harina*).

6. The French word *capote* 'coat' spread to Koasati and Alabama but not to Choctaw. A number of other loans from French are limited to the Koasati branch of Muskogean (see Kimball 1991:474). I am interested here in the spread of loanwords between branches of the family.

7. Haas (1941) identifies additional sets in which Western Muskogean Š corresponds to Eastern *c*. She has since discarded this correspondence (Haas 1969:38).

8. Haas's (1941) *i:o* correspondence was reconstructed as * . . . *iku* by Haas (1969:50), and as * . . . *ixo* by Nicklas in unpublished work.

9. Nicklas (personal communication) reports that some Choctaw speakers have falling tone on the penultimate syllable in 'three' and 'five'.

10. For additional evidence of Siouan-Muskogean contact, see Nicklas (1979b) and Rankin (1980).

Mobilian Jargon in the "Prehistory" of Southeastern North America

Emanuel J. Drechsel

As recently as the 1950s there survived among Louisiana Indians, Alabama-Coushatta of eastern Texas, and their non-Indian neighbors a Native American contact language by the name of Mobilian Jargon, also known as the Chickasaw-Choctaw trade language. Throughout colonial times it served as the major interlingual medium among linguistically diverse Indians of southeastern North America and in their contacts with immigrant Europeans and Africans. In its geographic range, Mobilian Jargon covered much of greater colonial Louisiana from Alabama to eastern Texas, extended probably into Georgia and central Florida, and reached from the Mississippi delta region as far north as southern, perhaps central, Illinois and apparently some five hundred miles up the Missouri River during its peak periods in the eighteenth and the first half of the nineteenth centuries. This area was the home of native peoples who spoke numerous mutually unintelligible, structurally diverse languages belonging to several distinct linguistic families, especially Muskogean, non-Muskogean Gulf isolates, Caddoan, Siouan, Algonquian, and likely others, including presently unidentified languages. In post-Columbian times, European and African immigrants introduced several distinct languages into the region, including Spanish, French, English, German, French- and English-based pidgins-creoles, and perhaps a few African languages as well.

As ethnically and linguistically diverse as the speakers of Mobilian Jargon were, just as varied were the contexts in which the language could be heard. Mobilian Jargon was an integral part of many traditional southeastern Indian societies in colonial times, and in fact it survived the longest in the culturally most conservative native communities of the Southeast; namely, among the Alabama, Coushatta, Choctaw, and their associates in Louisiana and eastern Texas. For these Indians, Mobilian Jargon not only served as an interlingual contact medium, it also fulfilled a valuable buffer function: it kept non-Indian outsiders at a social distance while reconfirming the speakers' identity as Indians in a racist environment (Drechsel 1987).

In terms of its linguistic structure, Mobilian Jargon reflects the influence of Muskogean and perhaps other Gulf languages (such as Tunica, Natchez, Chitimacha, and Atakapa). The phonology is principally Muskogean and includes the lateral fricative [£], but reveals no complex morphophonemic alterations. Without inflectional morphology, Mobilian Jargon is typologically analytic and exhibits the unusual word order X/OsV and possibly X/OSV.[1] This first pattern actually corresponds to the word order in Muskogean and other Gulf languages in which certain "subject" pronouns function as prefixes to the verb, and the object in turn precedes the entire verbal construction, thus resulting in Os-V (with the hyphen indicating that the "subject" pronoun is bound to the verb). Lexically, Mobilian Jargon draws much on Choctaw but incorporates words from other Muskogean languages and northern Algonquian languages, and a few words from Spanish, French, and English. The medium varied considerably in its lexical composition depending on its speakers, however; by all indications it was not mutually intelligible with any of the speakers' native languages, including Choctaw.

Sociolinguistically, Mobilian Jargon meets all the requirements of the definition of a stable pidgin; that is, a socially accepted interlingual compromise serving as an auxiliary medium in multilingual environments (Mühlhäusler 1986:5). In this case, *jargon* is only part of the pidgin's name. It has no implications in terms of an individual makeshift or ad hoc response in restricted interlingual communication without established syntactic rules, as the term is often used nowadays in pidgin and creole studies (e.g., Mühlhäusler 1986:135–47). In its sociolinguistic nature, Mobilian Jargon instead corresponds to another, better known American Indian pidgin, namely Chinook Jargon of the Pacific Northwest (Thomason 1983; Drechsel 1981).

QUESTIONS OF MOBILIAN JARGON'S ORIGIN:
PRE-EUROPEAN OR POSTCONTACT?

Whereas sociolinguistic-historical research in recent years has provided a reasonably solid understanding of Mobilian Jargon's structure and function, there remain many unresolved questions about its origin and development. This issue already occupied the minds of nineteenth-century scholars interested in Mobilian Jargon (such as the botanist Thomas Nuttall, the anthropologists Henry R. Schoolcraft and James Mooney, the ethnologist Albert S. Gatschet, and the Alabama historian Peter Joseph Hamilton), who assumed its use during the earliest periods of colonial explorations of greater Florida in the first part of the sixteenth century. These scholars apparently thought that Mobilian Jargon was already in existence when the first Spanish and French explorers set foot in southeastern North America. Americanists of the first half of the twentieth century such as John R. Swanton and William A. Read did not challenge their predecessors. They also believed that the pidgin was a native institution and implicitly suggested its aboriginal existence and pre-European origin.

In his survey of American Indian contact media, Michael Silverstein (1973:29–32) rejects the notion of a precolonial Mobilian Jargon, although he offers no contradictory evidence. In reviewing the evidence in support of Mobilian Jargon's pre-European existence, James M. Crawford (1978:21–29) similarly argues against such a hypothesis. Both authors argue for the origin of Mobilian Jargon as a result of French colonialism in Louisiana, and they do so on the basis of absent attestations or other sociolinguistic indications for the pidgin before the beginning of the eighteenth century.

Silverstein's and Crawford's arguments, however, present a poor case and retain little validity in light of additional evidence and from a broader sociolinguistic-sociohistorical perspective (see Drechsel 1984 for major counterarguments). In their reasoning, Silverstein and Crawford also neglect to address several fundamental questions related to Mobilian Jargon's origin: Why, in the first place, did European explorers and settlers make any effort to adopt an American Indian medium in what they considered their colonies? Why did Spanish, French, and English not become the Europeans' dominant *lingue franche* in their interactions with the Indians of the South until the twentieth century?

Why was Mobilian Jargon not relexified into a contact medium with a predominantly European vocabulary early in colonial history as happened in European colonies elsewhere on the globe? Why did relexification take place in the case of Mobilian Jargon only some two centuries later when its eastern variety, known as the lingua franca Creek (Drechsel 1983), apparently became relexified into Seminole Pidgin English? The sociolinguistic facts of the colonial South simply do not match the sociopolitical realities of the Indians' submission, exploitation, slavery, and extermination by European colonists. A convincing answer to this sociolinguistic-sociopolitical discrepancy appears all the more crucial in light of the fact that Spanish, French, and English, although frequently pidginized and creolized, became the dominant languages of colonized non-European peoples elsewhere in the world.

The only simple and straightforward answer suggests that the pidgin already existed across extended regions and among most native peoples of southeastern North America at the time the first Europeans arrived. In other words, it had originated in pre-Columbian times. Native peoples competent in Mobilian Jargon conveniently extended its use to the European newcomers rather than embracing any of their languages as contact media. Conversely, learning widely used Mobilian Jargon proved more practical, if not economical, for early Spanish and French explorers and colonists than attempting to impose their own languages on the native population, and thus set a precedent for later immigrants. In adopting Mobilian Jargon, there would have been no need for Europeans to recognize its true functions as an interlingual medium; they could have used it in the belief that its simplicity suited the presumably simple-minded Indians better than their own "civilized" European languages.

Yet neither the rejection of Silverstein's and Crawford's arguments nor questions about Mobilian Jargon's sociolinguistic-sociopolitical discrepancy qualifies as evidence for the pre-European origin of Mobilian Jargon, which obviously requires positive support in some form or another. Such an approach requires a broad range of considerations, including extralinguistic data and findings from archaeology. Only through such a comprehensive approach can we hope to answer the question of Mobilian Jargon's origin.

ARGUMENTS IN SUPPORT OF MOBILIAN JARGON'S
PRE-COLUMBIAN ORIGIN

At closer examination, there are several indications that Mobilian Jargon was in use before Europeans arrived in North America. Its linguistic nature, its functional pervasiveness, and its widespread use in early colonial periods with few or no limits to its sociolinguistic contexts speak for the hypothesis that the pidgin was not a secondary or incidental phenomenon of colonial origin but a well-established native institution of considerable age and with a pre-European ancestry (Drechsel 1984).

Mobilian Jargon not only has a predominantly Native American and primarily Muskogean vocabulary, it also has a distinct and rare syntactic pattern without structural parallels in any of the known languages of recent immigrants to North America. The pidgin's word order of X/OsV and possibly a rare and exotic concomitant of X/OSV in fact echo characteristic Muskogean and even Proto-Muskogean patterns, whose history extends back into pre-Columbian times. Mobilian Jargon reveals a striking syntactic analogy with Western Muskogean languages, as illustrated in the examples of Choctaw and Chickasaw shown in Figure 1.[2]

According to Pamela Munro and Lynn Gordon (1982:83), speakers of Western Muskogean use pronominal prefixes in constructions with the second person singular of active verbs, the first and second person singular of patient verbs, and all three singular persons of experiencer verbs, which could be preceded by an object or adverbial phrase. Similarly, Mary Haas (1946b:326–27) has described Choctaw active verbs and one of the three active-verb classes in Koasati, an Eastern Muskogean language, as exhibiting a pattern of verbal prefixes for the second person singular and plural subject pronouns as well as the first person plural subject pronoun (with the first person singular subject pronoun consisting of a suffix and the third person subject, singular and plural, remaining morphologically unmarked). Haas (1946b:331, 1969:54–55) has even suggested the same pattern for one of the three active-verb classes in Proto-Muskogean and for the conjugation of active verbs in pre-Proto-Muskogean except for the third person, which remains internally nonreconstructable (Figure 2).

Ultimately, these reconstructions of the Muskogean verbal pronouns may even be related to an analogous grammatical pattern in two

'You saw a man'.

Mobilian Jargon	*hattak	eSno	taha.	pesa
	'man'	'you'	'see'	PAST
Choctaw	hattak	iS-	pisa	tuk.
	'man'	2nd sing. subject prefix for active verbs	'see'	PAST

'I forgot the song'.

Mobilian Jargon	*talowa	eno	emehakse	taha.
	'song'	'I'	'forget'	PAST
Chickasaw	talowa'	am-	alhkaniya	-tok
	'song'	1st sing. subject prefix for experiencer verbs	'forget'	PAST

Fig. 1. Mobilian Jargon analogous with western Muskogean sentences (from Jacob et al. 1977:65; and Munro and Gordon 1982:85).

	Proto-Muskogean	*Pre-Proto-Muskogean*
1st sing.	*-li	*verb stem + li
2nd sing.	*iš-	*iS + verb stem
3rd sing.	*∅	*verb stem
1st pl.	*il(i)-	*ili + verb stem
2nd pl.	*haš(i)-	*haS + verb stem
3rd pl.	*∅	*verb stem

Fig. 2. Verbal pronouns in Proto-Muskogean and pre-Proto-Muskogean as reconstructed by Mary Haas (1946b:331 and 1969:54–55).

Gulf isolates; specifically, subject prefixes in Natchez auxiliaries and Tunica periphrastic constructions (Haas 1956:71–72, 1977). All these instances, however, exhibit a pattern in which an independent subject, a direct or indirect object, some adverbial phrase, or possibly even an entire clause preceded the verb—including any prefixed pronoun—in contrast to varying patterns of alternating verbal prefixes and suffixes in the descendant Muskogean languages. In the assumption that objects and probably also adverbial phrases introduced Proto-Muskogean and pre-Proto-Muskogean verbal constructions in analogy to the pattern of their modern descendant forms, the basic word order of ancestral Muskogean languages was Os-V, thus serving as an early syntactic model for Mobilian Jargon. In other words, the characteristic OsV word order of Mobilian Jargon echoes a pre-Columbian pattern of distinctly Proto-Muskogean and even pre-Proto-Muskogean verbal paradigms. Any alternative explanation would be far less satisfactory, for one would then have to find an answer to the question of why Mobilian Jargon speakers chose such a highly marked word order of X/OsV and possibly X/OSV in light of variable and less marked Muskogean and other Gulf models, for which there appears to be no obvious reply.

On the other hand, if one accepts the arguments in favor of the initial position of objects and perhaps adverbial phrases, the pronominal root of Mobilian Jargon's proposed basic word order of X/OsV and possibly X/OSV further suggests the hypothesis that the pidgin developed with pronominal constructions rather than with sentences including nouns as subjects. This inference would indeed seem quite reasonable. Conversations in early Mobilian Jargon, a contact medium, likely involved not abstract reasoning but the day-to-day interpersonal affairs and immediate environment of speakers and audience. The subject, either a known entity or old information to the audience, could then be easily expressed by tacit person deixis; that is, by a pronoun rather than a full noun. Haas's reconstructed comparative evidence suggests a greater time depth for the history of Mobilian Jargon than hitherto assumed by anthropologists of the nineteenth and early twentieth centuries. Such reconstructive reasoning does not necessarily require any phonological correspondences between Mobilian Jargon subject pronouns and their Proto-Muskogean or pre-Proto-Muskogean counterparts. In its long history (possibly several centuries) the pidgin probably underwent a relexification, perhaps several, reflecting the changes in the dominant influence of different native-language groups.

Surpassed in linguistic diversity only by the inhabitants of native California and the Pacific Northwest, southeastern Indians were linguistically heterogeneous enough in North America to encourage the development of an intertribal contact medium. Evidence from their post-Columbian descendants indicates that the indigenous population of the Southeast spoke languages of several distinct linguistic families (Muskogean, Caddoan, Siouan, Algonquian, and Iroquoian), various Gulf and other isolates, and numerous other, unidentified, languages (see Crawford 1975; Haas 1971, 1973, 1979b). Mobilian Jargon did not require the stimulus of recent immigrants from Europe or Africa for its development.

Mobilian Jargon's cumulative geographic range across the middle South, from northern Florida to eastern Texas and the upper Mississippi River valley, provides further support for its pre-European origin, for the pidgin's colonial distribution closely matches the geography of the pre-Columbian Mississippians, a system of complex chiefdoms distinguished by rudiments of a nascent civilization.[3] The early Mississippians formed a network of more or less stable intertribal alliances and over time came to adopt many common cultural traditions characteristic of much of the native Southeast. In spite of considerable cultural uniformity, southeastern Indians undoubtedly included representatives of all the major language families and isolates of the greater Southeast, and they must have maintained bi- and multilingual communities with distinct, frequently unrelated languages if their colonial period descendants provide any indication. The linguistic diversity of southeastern Indians in contrast with their cultural uniformity has constituted an unresolved dilemma (Crawford 1975:1–2) to which scholars of southeastern Indians have paid insufficient attention until today, but for which the hypothesis of Mobilian Jargon as an intertribal medium of the pre-Columbian Mississippian Complex would offer an elegant solution.

Indian speakers of the pidgin also revealed attitudes toward it that differed from those of non-Indians, especially Europeans, toward pidgins or other contact languages based on their own languages. In colonial times, the pidgin was a standard medium in traditional southeastern Indian societies used widely by the sociopolitical elite, including native diplomats. The speakers' former requirement for a positive disposition toward their counterparts reveals a unique sociolinguistic perspective, explainable in terms of long-term native traditions and possibly reflecting an indigenous origin rather than European contact. If Mobilian Jargon were a postcontact phenomenon, and if the southeastern Indians intended a positive disposition toward Europeans and their American descendants, one would expect them to have made some effort to switch from Mobilian Jargon to Spanish, French, or English, all of which native interpreters had learned since the first contacts with Europeans. One would also have to explain why southeastern Indians promoted a positive attitude toward the colonists, whom they clearly recognized as usurpers from the earliest colonial periods. That southeastern Indians instead thought of Mobilian Jargon as an institution of their own transpires from its early descriptions as a "mother language" or a kind of ancestral language, as offered by Jean Benjamin Francois Dumont de Montigny (1747:430; 1753, 1:181–82), Bernard Romans (1962 [1775]:59), and a French settler with the surname Berquin-Duvallon (1803:191). In his *Histoire de la Louisiane*, Antoine Simon Le Page du Pratz (1758, 3:89) specifically cites an older Yazoo Indian named Moncacht-apé who thought the Chickasaw to be the Yazoos' elders because "c'est d'eux que vient la Langue du Pays (la Langue vulgaire;)"; that is, Mobilian Jargon. If we can trust such attestations as reliable historical sources, Moncacht-apé referred to the common language of his and the Chickasaws' ancestors, both of whom apparently were members of the Mississippian Complex.

These observations are speculations, but they provide a reasonable model of how southeastern Indians interacted with one another in pre-Columbian times. None of the arguments offered in support can on its own make a strong case for the pidgin's pre-European origin, but in combination they provide a convincing foundation for this hypothesis. The absence of any contradictory or better evidence warrants an examination of Mobilian Jargon as possible lingua franca of the Mississippian Complex as reconstructed on the basis of archaeological data and vestiges of ethnographic evidence among post-Columbian southeastern Indians.

MOBILIAN JARGON: THE LINGUA FRANCA OF THE MISSISSIPPIAN COMPLEX?

The archaeological and ethnohistorical information available on pre-Columbian southeastern Indians obviously cannot yield any conclusive information on how they spoke with one another, but it permits enough reconstruction of the broader sociocultural context to explore the kinds of sociolinguistic situations in which Mobilian Jargon could feasibly have functioned as their major lingua franca.

At the center of precolonial southeastern North America was the Mississippian Complex, also known as the Southeastern or Southern Ceremonial Complex, Southern Cult, and others, consisting of a more or less integrated system of interacting and complex chiefdoms across much of the eastern deciduous woodlands with its heartland in the central Mississippi Valley.[4] At times presumed descendants of a Meso-American civilization because of superficial cultural similarities, Mississippians exhibited the most complex sociopolitical organizations in native North America from at latest A.D. 900 into protohistoric times—that is, the period of the early sixteenth century until approximately 1700. But the Mississippian Complex did *not* constitute a civilization in the anthropological sense; member groups lacked the sociopolitical integration of a state (i.e., a complex society consisting of urban centers with a surrounding and supportive hinterland) and dealt with one another as much by armed conflict as by economic cooperation including trade.

Mississippian settlements usually were located in major river floodplains on levees or bluffs, and they exploited fertile environments for growing crops; gathering natural products of the bottomlands, forests, and swamps (such as fruit, berries, nuts, seeds, roots, and tubers); and for other natural resources such as fish, migrating waterfowl, and game. Mississippians subsisted essentially on intensive agriculture and cultivated a variety of crops, including maize, beans, and squash, but increasingly came to rely on maize, which constituted up to 50 percent of their diet. These peoples distinguished themselves not only by improved farming methods but also by a more sophisticated technology, numerous innovations, and a rich artistry evident in various artifacts, including chipped flint, ground and polished stone, engraved and excised shells, elaborate ceramics, and embossed copper plates. Judging by the attention Mississippians paid to their arts and crafts, skilled artisans probably enjoyed considerable recognition and high status among their people.

Rich environments and greater reliance on food production (in contrast to hunting and gathering) yielded a considerable surplus and permitted a substantial growth in the population, which became increasingly sedentary over time, as reflected in the development of permanent settlements and larger, more complex aggregations of people. Mississippians lived in communities varying in size from hamlets inhabited by an extended family to towns with several thousand inhabitants. Whatever their size, these communities did not constitute separate sociopolitical entities; they were parts of a larger network covering extended regions in which farmsteads and subsidiary villages fed natural and other resources to larger communities or towns. These regional polities formed complex chiefdoms (i.e., hierarchical societies with ranked communities) in which towns exerted a dominant role as political and ceremonial centers, evident from larger public buildings (such as council houses), town squares, and earthen platform or temple mounds. At various times there emerged regional centers of political and religious power—as, for instance, at Moundville near Tuscaloosa, Alabama, and at Cahokia east of St. Louis, which had populations as large as 2000–5000 persons (in the latter case perhaps up to 10,000) during their peak periods. A growing population and larger sedentary aggregations also resulted in increased social differentiation and stratification with emergent classes of commoners and an elite, as reflected in differences in burial practices, diet, and health. The elite consisted of centralized political authorities in control of the resources and a religious leadership in charge of elaborate ceremonial traditions and, apparently, a widespread shared belief system, suggested by a rich iconography on artifacts.

Increasing numbers of people, competition for limited resources, the development of larger polities, and greater social fragmentation and stratification led to strife within and between regional associations of villages and towns. Whereas member groups, like their "historic" descendants, probably acted out their differences in contests such as stickball games (comparable to lacrosse), the archaeological evidence of fortified settlements, projectile points in human bones and other injuries resulting from violence, and scenes of conflict portrayed on various artifacts also attests an established tradition of armed conflict and warfare, and even suggests the existence of war captives, vassals, and an elite of warrior chiefs. Bellicose Mississippians clearly attempted to control weaker neighbors, but apparently they did not use their power to expand their territory in a truly colonialist fashion. Intertribal political alliances remained fragile by all indications, and Mississippian sociopolitical integration ultimately did not give rise to a civilization. Nonetheless, Americanist archaeologists and ethnologists have long been puzzled by the question of how the Mississippians developed considerable sociocultural uniformity and expanded the so-called Southeastern Ceremonial Complex across much of central North America and beyond within a period of only a few hundred years. The question remains unanswered but has led archaeologists to suggest various models of diffusion-interaction and cultural colonization (B. Smith 1984).

A major integrating factor was trade. It placed Mississippians right at the center of an elaborate network of exchange across eastern North America extending from the Atlantic Coast to the Rocky Mountains and from the Gulf of Mexico to the Great Lakes. James B. Griffin (1990:9–10), dean of eastern North American archaeology, recognizes a far-reaching trade of numerous raw materials (such as salt, marine shells, flint, and copper) and manufactured goods (including pottery, shell gorgets, embossed copper plates, sculptured human figures, and human effigy and catlinite pipes). Trade in wood and food, difficult to document, he presumes to have occurred primarily at times of local droughts, floods, and other natural disasters such as tornadoes or hurricanes. Although he expresses doubt about the occurrence of trade at regular established intervals and the existence of a class of traders, Griffin (1990:10–11) believes that "trade was one of the activities that served both to reflect and to produce the distinct 'world' view that identifies most of the southeastern Mississippian societies as a large interacting culture area." Nonetheless, given its significance and wide range, trade among Mississippians and with their neighbors has received surprisingly little systematic attention until recently, and it still remains poorly understood according to the authors of a recent essay on this subject (J. Brown et al. 1990).

The sociocultural uniformity of Mississippians cannot hide geographic and temporal variations that may reflect greater differences among them than the archaeological evidence can attest. Within the Mississippian Complex there existed several regions, each with its own political and ceremonial center and with distinct traditions of its own, as reflected by variations in material culture and symbolism.

Foremost among their differences must have been their languages, which undoubtedly included representatives of all the major language families attested in eastern North America in modern times and probably others that have either remained unidentified or become extinct. Americanists of southeastern North America have frequently thought of the Mississippians as Muskogeans. Marion Johnson Mochon (1972) has even used lexical reconstruction to argue that—by greater differentiation of the semantic domains of subsistence, economy, sociopolitical organization, and worldview—Muskogean languages match archaeological interpretations of Mississippian culture better than the comparatively underdifferentiated vocabularies of Siouan languages of the Mississippi Valley. She specifically recognizes cognates and possible cognates for vegetable foods, the basic domesticate of corn, hoe technology, male leadership, concerns with solar movements, and purification in Choctaw and Muskogee (Muskogean) in contrast to a minimal set of cognates pertaining to food, shelter, and basic numbers in Biloxi, Ofo, and Osage (Siouan). But Mochon's reasoning is not convincing. Unfortunately, the lexical data available for the different languages are uneven in quantity and quality. Moreover, the author neglected to take into consideration the problem of language death and other sociolinguistic complications (related, for example, to elicitation); she also ignored other major language families and isolates for comparison without giving any justification (Mochon 1972:478–83). Hence, Mochon's data and reconstructions at best show that there could have been Muskogeans among the Mississippians but do not exclude Mississippi Siouans or speakers of other southeastern languages.

There remains considerable doubt about the exclusive identification of the Mississippian Complex with the Muskogean language family because of its limited linguistic diversification, and hence short time depth, in comparison with Mississippian "prehistory" (see B. Smith 1984:21–25); a better candidate for the Mississippian language family would be Gulf, which includes Muskogean and the isolates of Atakapa, Chitimacha, Natchez, and Tunica, related to Proto-Muskogean. But there is no reason to assume that the Mississippians spoke only one language or any specific linguistic family, superfamily, or phylum; rather, they spoke diverse languages that were not necessarily related. In fact, early European explorers still noted a great linguistic diversity among descendants of Mississippians such as the Illinois and probably other Algonquians, Muskogeans, the Natchez (Gulf) and linguistically unidentified affiliates, Caddoans, Siouans, and possibly Cherokee (Iroquoians).

The archaeological record of the Mississippian Complex suggests a variety of possible bi- and multilingual contexts: extensive and widespread trade in natural resources and products, multilingual complex chiefdoms, intertribal diplomacy and alliances, competition between neighboring communities in the form of games, intertribal religious and other ceremonies, enslavement of captives from raids on neighboring groups, and perhaps even some form of indigenous colonialism. The reconstruction of possible sociolinguistic contexts for Mississippians looks remarkably similar to those attested in historical and ethnographic records. In this case, there is little danger of circular reasoning. Although the interpretation of archaeological data has in part drawn on historical and ethnographic evidence, the data are themselves sufficiently detailed and reliable enough to allow no alternative interpretation.

If there existed any major differences between pre-Columbian and postcontact bi- and multilingual contexts, the intertribal interactions of Mississippians likely were sociolinguistically *more* complex (instead of less) than those of their colonial descendants—due to larger populations, greater linguistic diversity among them, and probably more frequent and institutionalized interactions as a result of their sociopolitical integration into large chiefdoms before the arrival of Europeans. Mississippians were linguistically diverse enough, however, and interacted with each other on a sufficiently regular basis and in a variety of contexts to warrant the hypothesis that Mobilian Jargon was used among them; they did not have to wait for European explorers and colonists to arrive before developing a contact medium. By introducing their own languages, "historic" immigrants could, however, have restored some of the aboriginal sociolinguistic diversity lost as a result of interrelated factors including newly introduced diseases, rapid population decline, and sociopolitical disintegration.

In light of the great linguistic diversity but considerable sociocultural uniformity among southeastern Indians, there arises the question of how their pre-Columbian ancestors, speaking so many different languages, interacted with each other in trade and other "intertribal" situations. Moreover, how did Mississippians and their descendants come to adopt so many sociocultural similarities while maintaining great linguistic differences?

With regard to exchange of materials, one could argue for the existence of silent trade. But silent interactions between speakers of different languages would have resulted in serious limitations in the established and far-reaching trade among the Mississippians, and would mostly be inoperable in contexts other than trade. On the other hand, Griffin (1990:10) surmises, probably by analogy with the early colonial situation, that native traders dealt with one another by relying on a knowledge of several languages. While this assumption seems quite reasonable in individual cases from the perspective of post-Columbian and especially postremoval history, with its references to intertribal and multilingual communities, it ultimately cannot explain the great linguistic diversity and sociopolitical integration among Mississippians. Large segments in their communities likely spoke several languages.

A simple and elegant answer to this communication problem would be the use of Mobilian Jargon as a contact language, in trade and in other interactions. The pidgin in some form comparable to modern attestations would have suited perfectly as a contact medium among Mississippians speaking different languages and could have served in other contexts than just those mentioned above. If we can take Mochon's list of Choctaw and Muskogee words related to subsistence, economy, sociopolitical organization, and worldview as a linguistic indicator for the Mississippian Complex, the pidgin would qualify as a suitable interlingual medium. Out of a total of 108 terms, the historically attested vocabulary of Mobilian Jargon (with fewer entries than the other languages except Ofo) could match a majority of words—at least 75 equivalent or corresponding terms, and in many instances with 2 or more equivalent or corresponding words—in contrast with the fewer comparable entries in Osage (70), Ofo (39), and Biloxi (46) listed by Mochon (1972:483–98).[5]

This pre-Columbian variety of Mobilian Jargon would not necessarily have to resemble recently recorded lects, but it could conceivably have exhibited considerable linguistic differences from any of the historically attested examples. Because of the possibility of repeated relexifications, it would, in fact, be outright misleading to assume that Mississippians spoke a predominantly Muskogean-based variety of Mobilian Jargon; thus there is no need to fear that the Mississippian-Muskogean identification will be reintroduced through the back door. Any Mississippian variety would likely have reflected the influence of its speakers' first languages in its phonology, lexicon, and possibly syntax as well. Assuming that Mississippians spoke languages other than just some Muskogean ones, we would have to expect Caddoan Mississippians to have shown substantial Caddoan elements in their version of the pidgin, and people of Cahokia perhaps an Algonquian-influenced lect. Mobilian Jargon, as we know it in its modern forms, possibly dominated only in Muskogia's heartland—the greater region of Moundville in Alabama. We must even be prepared to recognize that such different varieties were not always mutually intelligible and that Mobilian Jargon was not the only contact medium in the Mississippian Complex.

Like any of its modern varieties, however, a pre-Columbian Mobilian

Jargon need not have been subject to any structural-functional restrictions and could have met all the communicative demands of Mississippians. For all practical purposes, its speakers could have held conversations with each other on any topic and in any context. The pidgin could further have functioned as the very language of vassals among southeastern Indians, a possibility a recent speaker invoked by calling it *yoka anompa* 'slave/servant language'. Linguistically, Mobilian Jargon also matched the sociopolitical integration of complex chiefdoms—by nature dynamic and flexible but also rather unstable societies. The pidgin provided a common medium while allowing its speakers to maintain their native languages and with them their social identities as they did in colonial times (Drechsel 1987).

The results of research on Mobilian Jargon call into question any simplistic identification of a language group with any sociopolitical entity such as *tribe,* as is still customary in much of Americanist anthropology; instead, studies suggest bi- and multilingual communities with rather complex sociolinguistic arrangments whose members were undoubtedly multilingual but frequently did not share a knowledge of the same languages, especially when dealing with distant partners. An answer in terms of multilingualism thus appears insufficient and calls for a supplementary explanation such as Mobilian Jargon's use as a lingua franca. Mobilian Jargon served as an ideal and highly adaptive medium in rather unstable partnerships among larger kinship groups such as clans and moieties (Knight 1990) and other alliances across language boundaries. The pidgin actually mirrors the sociopolitical phenomenon of associated towns that brought together different southeastern Indian groups in response to disaster (such as crop failure, epidemic diseases, and military defeat) and that resulted in bi- and multilingual communities in recent history as apparently they did in pre-Columbian times. Aware of Mobilian Jargon's role, William S. Willis, Jr. (1980:100, 102) has already suggested that "twin towns helped spread pidgin languages. If so, the popularity of Mobilian [Jargon] as a lingua franca in the eighteenth century need not be explained entirely in terms of commercial and political relations between Indians and whites. . . . If ethnic and sociopolitical unity did not exist in multiple mound sites, then these prehistorical settlements also encouraged the linguistic processes of diffusion, bilingualism, polylingualism, and pidginization." In short, Mobilian Jargon is an example of peer-polity interaction: regular and systematic relationships between neighboring but politically autonomous groups across a larger area resulting in structural homologies (Renfrew and Cherry 1986).

Pressures toward a single national language would probably have increased only if the Mississippian Complex had developed into a state-level society, in which case a corresponding sociolinguistic centralization might have occurred with the selection of one language over others or possibly by a creolized Mobilian Jargon replacing the others as the community's primary language. But Mississippian chiefdoms did not evolve into a civilization, and Mobilian Jargon did not creolize. Nevertheless, the pidgin remains a possible vestige of the Mississippian Complex. French or English words of Mobilian Jargon origin such as *bayou* (Mobilian Jargon *bayok* 'creek, river'), even if perhaps never pronounced by pre-Columbian Mississippians, may provide as much of a historical link to them as their mounds, artifacts, and bones.

The notion of Mobilian Jargon as the lingua franca of the Mississippian Complex remains a hypothesis, as does the idea of the pidgin's pre-European origin. Ultimately, some conclusive historical evidence would be necessary to demonstrate it. For instance, one might hope for a document from the earliest contact of Europeans, specifically Spaniards, with southeastern Indians in which the latter report about the long-term, pre-Columbian use of an established lingua franca among Mississippians speaking diverse languages and also provide supportive sociolinguistic details of the structure, functions, and geographic range of the "international" medium. Archival research has not furnished such a paper thus far, and the chance of finding one seems remote in light of the fact that Spanish explorers and colonists of North America paid disappointingly little attention to native traditions, including ways of speaking.

NOTES

This essay builds on an earlier essay (Drechsel 1984) but incorporates new evidence and additional arguments. I discuss the subject further in chapter 11 of my forthcoming book *Mobilian Jargon: Linguistic and Sociohistorical Aspects of an American Pidgin* (tentative title). Over the years, I have drawn on valuable insights by several individuals, especially the late James M. Crawford, Hiram F. ("Pete") Gregory, George Huttar, William Samarin, and Sarah G. Thomason. Acknowledgment is also due to the University Research Council of the University of Hawai'i at Mānoa, which supported my participation at the keynote symposium "The Southeast at the Time of Columbus: Evidence from Linguistics and Archaeology," held in St. Augustine, Florida. The responsibility for the views expressed remains entirely my own.

1. *X* stands for indirect objects and adverbial phrases, *O* for a direct object, lowercase *s* for a pronominal subject, capital *S* for a nominal subject, and *V* for the verb.

2. The star below marks sentences in Mobilian Jargon reconstructed to match their Choctaw and Chickasaw counterparts word for word. Although not recorded in actual speech, these sentences follow the grammatical conventions of historical and modern examples.

3. I owe this observation to Hiram Gregory, who first pointed out in surprise how closely Mobilian Jargon and the Mississippian Complex overlapped in their geographic distributions.

4. I prefer and retain the term Mississippian Complex, even though it is not fashionable currently, because it makes an implicit and quite appropriate reference to a *multifaceted system of different interacting parts,* namely, smaller member groups with traditions of their own. Other designations focus unduly on the South or religion, suggest a sociocultural monolith that it was not, or carry negative implications. For simplicity's sake, however, I call its peoples Mississippians—with the explicit understanding that the term refers to diverse pre-Columbian inhabitants of the greater Mississippi Valley (i.e., the drainage of the Mississippi River) instead of the residents of the modern state with the same name.

The following paragraphs draw substantially on useful and recent synopses on the Mississippian Complex by James B. Griffin (1990) and Bruce D. Smith (1985). For further information, readers should examine the growing literature on the subject; for example, Dye and Cox (1990), Emerson and Lewis (1991), Galloway (1989), and B. Smith (1978, 1990) have made major recent contributions.

5. Among the 108 terms used by Mochon for her lexical reconstruction, Mobilian Jargon could match words for at least the following: *plant/to plant, wild potato, corn, beans, squash, field, farm, soil, to hoe, to till, to harvest, plate, pottery/pot, bowl,* and *bottle* (semantic domain of food production); *artisan, tribute/tax, to trade, to buy, to sell, to purchase, market/marketplace,* and *measure* (production and distribution); *nation, tribe, camp, village, town, city,*

people, household, clan/lineage, noble, chief, artisan, tributary people, rich, and *poor* (settlement and social category); *governor, kingdom, chief, armor, battle, to war, tributary people,* and *law* (polity); *to build, house, council house, bone house,* and *temple* (public construction); *sun, moon, month, menses, eclipse, week, year, deity/god, medicine, priest, ball ground, one, two, three, eleven, twelve, thirteen, ten, twenty, thirty, one hundred, one thousand,* and *the period of "fire extinguished"* (worldview). The available historical documentation of the pidgin cannot confirm any equivalent or corresponding terms for the other 33 terms, but it is still incomplete. These terms are *grindstone, dish* (food production); *to barter* (production and distribution); *class, rank,* and *lord* (settlement and social category); *to rule, assembly, council, council house, to arm, warrior,* and *to conquer* (polity); *builder, mound,* and *mountain* (public construction); *world, hour, planet, religion, to fast, January, February, March, April, May, June, July, August, September, October, November,* and *December* (worldview). Whether or not Mobilian Jargon once had words for these concepts, its speakers could easily have borrowed or created such anew as necessary.

There remains, however, considerable doubt about the applicability of lexical-reconstructive methodology (developed in the tradition of the comparative method and based on the tree model of language diversification) to contact languages because of the widespread borrowing and lexical replacement among them, which is why I do not develop this line of inquiry any further here.

On the other hand, one might even be tempted to take Mochon's Muskogean data as indirect evidence for Mobilian Jargon as the lingua franca of the Mississippian Complex by arguing that the similarities between the Choctaw and Muskogee words, on the one hand, and Mobilian Jargon, on the other, resulted from the latter exerting a conservative role and also serving as a source for new vocabulary. Because of considerable lexical variation and possible relexifications, such reasoning is without any foundation and runs the undue risk of circularity.

The Art of War in the Sixteenth-Century Central Mississippi Valley

David H. Dye

At the time of European contact the central Mississippi alluvial valley was the site of chiefdoms that might best be described as polities engaged in bilateral alliances or mutually antagonistic hostilities. By the sixteenth century warfare had reached such a sophisticated level that communities were constrained to concentrate within fortified towns and villages. Rival or politically allied polities recognized, maintained, and vigorously defended sharply demarcated territorial boundaries.

In the following discussion I briefly address the nature of chiefly warfare that members of the Hernando de Soto entrada saw and described in the central Mississippi Valley. The sixteenth-century ethnohistorical record in the central Mississippi Valley is limited to the accounts of the de Soto expedition, and, unfortunately, the chroniclers described few polities with more than a passing reference.

From May 8 to September 10, 1541, March 1542 to June 5, 1542, and December 1542 to July 2, 1543, the Spanish expedition led by Hernando de Soto traveled through the central Mississippi Valley between the vicinity of southeastern Missouri and the mouth of the Arkansas River (Dye 1992; Hudson 1985; Hudson et al. 1989, 1990; T. Lewis 1902; D. Morse and Morse 1983, 1990; D. Morse 1991; Phillips et al. 1951:348–91; G. Smith 1990).[1] The four accounts of their peregrinations form the basis for much of our knowledge concerning native warfare at the time of European contact (Elvas 1922; Hernández de Biedma 1922; Rangel 1922; Varner and Varner 1951).[2]

The Hernando de Soto entrada witnessed and documented a political environment charged with hostilities. Chiefdoms were engaged in internecine conquest warfare with their neighbors across buffer zones or sharply demarcated boundaries. Populations of commoners and nobles, tethered to chiefly elites, were safely positioned within well-fortified towns. At the time of the de Soto expedition in the mid-sixteenth century a stalemate may have been reached in which the relative strengths of individual polities were well known and coordinated attacks were attempted only when the odds appeared favorable for the aggressor. The de Soto expedition provided the spark that ignited smoldering hostilities among neighboring polities by upsetting the fragile power balances that had been so carefully crafted through alliances based on kinship, prestige, goods exchange, and tribute relations. Thus, European forces brought about increased aggression and escalated hostilities in the Mississippi alluvial plain just as they did in other areas of the New World (Ferguson and Whitehead 1992).

Garcilaso (Varner and Varner 1951:487–89) noted that each central Mississippi Valley chiefdom was at war with its neighbors.[3] Paramount chiefs were either at war with all those who shared their boundaries or they were allied with one neighbor or neighbors against others. No one was neutral.

Expedition members recorded several direct and indirect observations of warfare. Although Garcilaso (Varner and Varner 1951:488) states that the Mississippians knew of only one kind of warfare, an ambush style of attack, his descriptions and later archaeological evidence of fortified towns strongly suggest that chiefs controlled forces capable of constructing, maintaining, assaulting, and interdicting defensively held positions. Fortified Mississippian towns in the central Mississippi Valley have been well documented in the archaeological record (Chapman 1980; Lafferty 1973; D. Morse and Morse 1983; Price and Griffin 1979; Price and Fox 1993; J. Williams 1964) and among historically known groups such as the Natchez (Tregle 1975:375) and Bayogoula (McWilliams 1981:61).

In fact, the Spaniards witnessed large-scale attacks in the central Mississippi Valley on four occasions. These planned and coordinated assaults fall under two general headings: land-based offensives aimed at fortified towns, and lacustrine/riverine strikes consisting of coordinated fleets of war canoes. The land-based offensives, aided by the Spanish, were aimed at traditional enemies: Casqui attacking Pacaha and Guachoya assaulting Anilco. Waterborne assaults were directed at the Spaniards as they manufactured four barges in which to cross the Mississippi River and later when they constructed seven brigantines to carry them down the Mississippi River and to New Spain.

The first act of terrestrial warfare mentioned in the accounts was more a rout than a battle. As the expedition approached the fortified civic-ceremonial center of the Pacaha polity, the Casquins and Spaniards mounted an attack against the largely undefended town and sacked it. The confrontation between the Spanish-Casquin force and Pacaha was recorded by the Fidalgo de Elvas (1922:122–25) and Garcilaso (Varner and Varner 1951:434–45). Rodrigo Rangel notes only that the chief of Casqui came to the Christians when the Spaniards were entering Pacaha and "entertained" them "bravely," presumably referring to their military capabilities (1922:139–40).

The conquistadors were told that Pacaha and Casqui had been "waging a severe war" against one another and that it had its roots far back in the past. Casqui and his parents, grandparents, and more remote ancestors had all waged war on the lords of Pacaha (Elvas 1922:119; Hernández de Biedma 1922:26–30; Rangel 1922:139; Varner and Varner 1951:434). The importance of the conflict between the two chiefdoms is apparent in the fact that warfare was one of the first topics brought up for discussion by Casqui when the Spaniards entered his polity. He asked de Soto for a sign or omen to consult for support in his wars, perhaps in the sense of an oracle (Hernández de Biedma 1922:27), underscoring the importance of ideological forces in Mississippian warfare.

Pacaha's main civic-ceremonial center, a large town consisting of five hundred "large and good houses" (Varner and Varner 1951:436), was on a plain (natural levee) near the polity frontier; a swamp to the west formed the political and geographical boundary with the neighboring province. The town was well stockaded with towers, and both the towers and the surrounding palisade held many loopholes for firing at attackers. A human-made ditch, for the most part full of water, surrounded the town (Elvas 1922:123; Hernández de Biedma 1922:28; Rangel 1922:139; Varner and Varner 1951:437).[4] According to Garcilaso the ditch or moat was ten to twelve fathoms deep and between forty and fifty feet wide.[5] The ditch was wide enough for two canoes to pass without touching and provided access to the Mississippi River by another ditch, perhaps a modification of a natural stream. The meander lake on which the town sat was also connected to the Mississippi River, probably by a distributary that drained into the Mississippi from the lake. Thus the inhabitants had access to the meander lake and the Mississippi River through an interconnected system of ditches and natural waterways. Additional large towns, also surrounded by stockades and presumably ditches connected to adjacent lakes or rivers, were located at a distance of half a league to a league from the main town.[6] When the Spanish entrada first entered the paramount chiefdom of Pacaha on June 29, 1541, a large force of Casquin warriors equipped with weapons and adorned with feather headdresses accompanied and marched ahead of the Spaniards. Led by the paramount chief of Casqui, the force included a large number of bearers carrying food and armed with bows and arrows. The combined Spanish-Casquin force attacked the main town in a wholesale assault, although Pacaha and most of the inhabitants had fled as de Soto and Casqui approached.

As the Casquin warriors advanced on the largely abandoned and defenseless town, they were afraid that the Pacahans, whom they thought might be hidden within the town, might ambush them. Elvas (1922:122) notes that many of the townspeople were captured but not killed, but according to Garcilaso more than 150 men were killed, many of them decapitated as a symbol of Casqui's victory, and their heads placed on lances or poles outside the temple doors, replacing the Casquin heads that had stood there previously. The Casquins scalped many of the Pacahans as evidence of their triumph (the scalp signified a great victory and served as vengeance for past injuries). The captured women and children of Pacaha were taken back to Casqui to be used as field laborers. The Casquins found a number of their own people working in the Pacahan fields; their feet had been injured to prevent escape (Varner and Varner 1951:437, 439).

The Casquins sacked the town, in particular the houses of the ruling elite, and desecrated the Pacahan temple on the large public plaza by plundering the ornaments and riches and smashing the sacred objects. Each of the wooden funerary chests that served as sepulchers for the elite dead was thrown to the ground and the bodies trampled and kicked with contempt and scorn. The Casquins wanted to burn the temple and the chiefly residences along with the entire town, but they resisted lest they anger de Soto, who indicated to them that he had plans to use the houses during the expedition's stay at Pacaha. In the town the conquistadors found numerous shields of raw cowhide (bison?; see Elvas 1922:122).

While the Casquins and the Spaniards ransacked the town, Pacaha and most of his people, some five to six thousand in all (Elvas 1922:125), crossed the Mississippi carrying much of their clothing in cane baskets and on rafts and sought refuge on an island barricaded and fortified with two rows of thick timbers around its circumference.

After five days in the Pacahan town the Spaniards and Casquins went in search of Pacaha. While traveling in concert with the expedition the Casquins formed a wing half a league wide and destroyed the crops they encountered. At this time of year (mid-summer) the destruction of crops would have had a particularly ruinous effect upon the subsistence economy.

To bring Pacaha to de Soto as he had promised, Casqui returned to his principal town on the Casqui River. He ordered sixty canoes to navigate the Mississippi River, while he marched overland with his warriors, who formed a vanguard, a battalion, and a rear guard as they went to join de Soto at Pacaha.

After joining forces, de Soto sent two hundred footmen in twenty of Casqui's canoes. Three thousand Casquin warriors embarked in the remaining forty canoes to attack Pacaha's island stronghold (Varner and Varner 1951:435, 440).[7] Antonio Osorio and four other Spaniards accompanied the Casquin warriors to determine how many people were on the island with Pacaha. De Soto, conducted by Casqui and his warriors, took forty horsemen and sixty footmen and headed overland from the town of Pacaha to the island.

According to Elvas the Pacahans mistook the Casquin flotilla for a Spanish armada and fled the island. De Soto sent his men across the river in Casquin canoes to join Osorio, who had already landed on the island with the Casquins. Pacaha and several others escaped in three canoes, and the remainder of his people either drowned trying to cross the Mississippi to the eastern side or remained on the island and were captured. The Casquins filled their canoes with the baskets full of clothing that floated down the Mississippi and returned to their hometowns with both captives and new clothes (Elvas 1922:124–25). In Garcilaso's version, Pacaha called a halt to the fighting in order to gain de Soto's favor when he saw that the Spaniards would be annihilated by his forces.

A second land assault took place in late April 1542. De Soto hoped to instill fear among the Guachoyan and Nilco people because he saw that his expedition was in a vulnerable position. The chiefdom of Nilco was the most populous province he had seen in the Southeast and except for Coosa and Apalachee had the most maize (Elvas 1922:149). Nilco's town comprised some four hundred houses surrounding a plaza or series of plazas; chiefly residences sat atop a high mound that dominated the town (Varner and Varner 1951:485).

Taking advantage of Nilco's and Guachoya's great hatred for each other and the fact that they were at war at the time of the Spaniards' visit (Elvas 1922:150, 156–58, 185; Hernández de Biedma 1922:34; Varner and Varner 1951:485–87, 492–95, 546), de Soto ordered Captain Juan de Guzmán to ascend the river of Nilco in war canoes with a company of footmen and four thousand Guachoyans who had been sent by their chief for a combined Guachoyan-Spanish dawn attack. De Soto with his men and Guachoya with two thousand warriors and a "great multitude" of Guachoyans to carry supplies traveled overland to rendezvous in three days with Guzmán on the riverbank across from Nilco (Varner and Varner 1951:492). Elvas, however, states that de Soto sent Captain Nuño de Tobar overland with fifteen horsemen to meet Guzmán, who arrived at the town first. In any event, the Spanish-Guachoyan force crossed the river at night and attacked the town at dawn; the forces captured eighty women and children. According to Elvas the Guachoyans filled their canoes with clothing looted from the houses and returned to their town to recount to their chief that the Spaniards had massacred the Nilcoans (Elvas 1922:156–58). Garcilaso, on the other hand, reports that the Guachoyans were the ones who butchered the inhabitants, placing their heads on lances at the temple doors and destroying the temple contents and sacred objects in much the same way as had been done at Pacaha. In this scenario the shocked Spaniards reported the Guachoyan atrocities to de Soto, who apparently did not witness the massacre (Varner and Varner 1951:492–95, 546).[8]

A third attack was planned by an interpolity alliance in the spring of 1543 while the new governor, Luys de Moscoso, was at the stockaded community of Aminoya, which comprised two neighboring towns (Elvas 1922:186), each of some two hundred houses. A ditch or moat connected to the Mississippi River encircled the towns, making an island of them (Varner and Varner 1951:531). Although the assault was not carried out, the organization evidenced by the attacking forces is informative for an understanding of Mississippi military strategy. Moscoso had learned from a captive that Quigualtam, the chief of a major polity on the eastern side of the Mississippi, was forming an alliance with the neighboring chiefs of Nilco, Guachoya, Taguanate, and others (in all, some twenty polities) in order to attack the Spaniards with a large force (Elvas 1951:189–90; Varner and Varner 1951:540, 560, 563). Hoping to conceal their purpose with false messages of friendship, the alliance sent some fish as a present to de Soto. On the day of the intended assault another present was to be sent in advance of the attack by bearers and servers who were to take possession of the Spaniards' lances, which they customarily placed near the doors of their dwellings. The houses would then be set on fire, and the chiefs and their forces, concealed in a thicket near the town, would attack on seeing the flames. Moscoso learned of the intended attack, however, and took decisive measures to thwart it. The ability of the various polities to become allies on such a large scale in the face of a common threat is quite instructive.

The de Soto expedition witnessed two incidents of well-orchestrated military maneuvers on the Mississippi River. The first took place from May 21 until June 17, 1541, when an imposing fleet of large, well-made war canoes attacked the Spaniards in Quizquiz province each afternoon as they were constructing four barges in which to cross the Mississippi River (Elvas 1922:113–14; Hernández de Biedma 1922:26; Rangel 1922:137–38; Varner and Varner 1951:428–29). Garcilaso states that there were 6000 canoes, but Hernández de Biedma suggests there were only 250.[9] Elvas likewise gives an account of 200 large dugouts. Rangel agrees with Elvas that there were 200 canoes and estimates the number of warriors as seven thousand; he also states that the attackers were Pacaha's men from upriver, but Elvas reports that they were vassals of a great lord named Aquixo whose polity was directly across the Mississippi River from Quizquiz (Elvas 1922:138, 112).[10]

Arranged in squadrons, the Mississippians traveled up and down the river, showering the Spaniards with arrows. They yelled insults at them and boasted of their prowess whenever they came abreast of the half-built barges. The warriors were painted with ochre and wore great bunches of white and colored plumes.[11] Standing warriors with bows and arrows held feathered shields on both sides of their canoes to shelter the oarsmen. The shields were constructed of canes so strong and closely interwoven that a crossbow could hardly pierce them. In one canoe an awning located at the poop provided shade for the paramount chief, who issued orders and directed the course of the other canoes. The raised platform not only allowed the chief to see the field of battle, it also elevated him above the field of commoner and elite warriors and maintained his ritual purity (Lankford 1992). Other individuals, perhaps chiefs of lesser rank or rulers of allied polities, had the same arrangement. The canoes carried banners "like a famous armada of galleys" (Elvas 1922:114) and retired each afternoon with great order. When the entrada crossed the Mississippi River on June 18, 1541, they avoided the native armada, which had so aggravated them each afternoon, by crossing at dawn.

The second incidence of riverine warfare took place when a fleet of Quigualtam canoes harassed the Spanish brigantines as they left Aminoya to descend the Mississippi for New Spain (Elvas 1922:196–201; Hernández de Biedma 1922:39; Varner and Varner 1951:571–89). The Quigualtams believed they were more powerful against the Spaniards on water than on land and therefore readied as many people and war dugouts as they could muster to pursue the Spaniards when they left Aminoya to go down the river, "for there they thought to slay them all" (Varner and Varner 1951:564). As is often the case, Elvas and Garcilaso differ in their interpretations of the events.

According to Elvas the expedition left Aminoya on July 2, 1543. On July 4, while the Spaniards were busy shelling corn in a small village near the riverbank, some Quigualtam warriors came up the river in war canoes and invited the Spaniards to match military skills with them. The Quigualtams "somewhat carelessly put themselves in order of battle" (1922:195) but fled when the Spaniards pursued them. Finding the Spaniards unable to overtake them, however, they turned and followed the Spaniards on land and in canoes and regrouped in a town near the river. The Spaniards routed the Quigualtam force and burned the town. This action of the Quigualtams may have been an exercise to test the Spaniards' prowess on water or to entice them into a trap by appearing somewhat careless and unorganized (1922:196–201).

Garcilaso states that on the morning of the second day a large fleet of war canoes began to follow the expedition, observing and assessing the strength of the Spanish forces. The Quigualtam fleet, with more than a thousand canoes amassed by several chiefs, mainly Quigualtam, greatly impressed the Spanish chroniclers; it was the largest and best assemblage of war canoes seen in the Southeast. The command canoes and others like them supported twenty-five paddlers on each side and held twenty-five or thirty warriors, who were placed in a row from one end to the other. The largest war canoes held seventy-five to eighty warriors.[12] The paddlers carried their own bows and arrows. The smallest canoes, slightly more than forty feet long and four feet wide, carried between forty and forty-five warriors. The paddles were two feet wide and between six feet and four and a half feet long. Each canoe, the paddles, and the men's equipment and clothing were painted a single color. Rowing simultaneously and in rhythm according to different songs, the speed depending on the tune, the men boasted of their war deeds and shouted insults. At the close of each song they gave tremendous shouts and cries. With all hands rowing at full strength, the vessels could be propelled as fast as a horse running at full speed (Varner and Varner 1951:571–76).

At noon of the second day the Quigualtam canoes separated into three equal groups—a vanguard, a battalion, and a rear guard—along the west bank of the river. The vanguard formed a long, narrow column and crossed the river in front of the Spanish fleet, shooting arrows at the Spaniards as they crossed. The vanguard then recrossed the river behind the Spanish brigantines as the battalion and then the rear guard fired at the entrada in turn.[13] Garcilaso describes the maneuver as a tournament of canes. The warriors shot volleys of arrows, attacking each of the seven brigantines one at a time. When the Spaniards used mats to protect themselves from the arrows, the Quigualtam warriors shot high into the air so that the arrows would fall on the hapless conquerors behind the walls. They discontinued the attack at the end of each day and began again at daybreak for ten consecutive days and nights (Varner and Varner 1951:577–79).

On the eleventh day the Quigualtam warriors spread out across the river behind the Spanish fleet and waited for stragglers. "Since the river was broad and they could spread out in all directions without breaking rank, they made a magnificent spectacle to behold" (Varner and Varner 1951:576). The canoes were so numerous that they covered the river from one bank to the other for a quarter of a league upriver.

Eventually one brigantine fell behind the other six. It was quickly overtaken by the Quigualtams, but they were forced to withdraw when the remaining brigantines went to the beleaguered ship's aid. For the next two days the Quigualtams followed less than a quarter of a league behind the Spanish fleet hoping to catch the Spaniards off-guard or to attack another straggler.

According to Garcilaso, on the sixteenth day Estévan Añez and five others drew away from the brigantines in a small dugout to attack the Quigualtam fleet. The governor ordered three canoes commanded by Juan de Guzmán to bring Añez and his companions back. As the four Spanish canoes approached, the Quigualtam fleet opened ranks to allow them to be entrapped. Once encircled, the right flank rammed the Spaniards' canoes and killed their occupants with arrows or paddles. Forty-eight of the fifty-two Spaniards in the four canoes were killed or captured, including the brigantine commander, Juan de Guzmán (Varner and Varner 1951:577–87).

Elvas records the events of the sixteenth day slightly differently. On July 7, one hundred canoes with sixty to seventy warriors in each approached from downriver, came within two crossbow shots of the Spaniards, and blocked their way.[14] Quigualtam's messengers advanced in a small canoe to learn the character of the Spanish vessels and weapons. After they withdrew, the messengers began shouting threats at the Spaniards. Moscoso sent Juan de Guzmán, captain of the footmen, and twenty-five men in armor in small canoes to drive the Quigualtams out of the way. As the Spaniards approached the Quigualtam flotilla it split into two parts, allowing the Spaniards to enter. They then closed in on Guzmán and his men, capsizing the canoes and striking the Spaniards' heads with canoe paddles and clubs (Elvas 1922:196–97).

At the boundary of Quigualtam's province his war canoes turned back and some fifty canoes from the adjoining (unnamed) province took up the chase.[15] At the end of their polity they turned back and seven canoes continued the pursuit (Elvas 1922:200–201).

Warfare throughout much of the Southeast was primarily a political, if not ideological, struggle among rival elites on both an intrapolity and interpolity level. When the Europeans arrived, community-level aggression comprised two basic components: raids on land by small warrior contingents, and large well-planned and coordinated attacks both on land and on water (Anderson 1990:151; DePratter 1983:45; Dye 1990:211). Garcilaso has this to say concerning warfare in the Southeast:

One should know that [warfare] was not a conflict of force against force with an organized army or with pitched battles, except in rare instances, or a conflict instigated by the lust and ambition of some lords to seize the estates of others. Their struggle was one of ambushes and subtlety in which

they attacked each other on fishing and hunting trips and in their fields and
along their roads wherever they could find an enemy off guard. And those
whom they seized on such occasions, they held as slaves, some in perpetual
bondage with one foot maimed, . . . and some as prisoners to be ransomed
and exchanged. But the hostility among these Indians amounted to no more
than the harm they inflicted upon their persons with deaths, wounds, and
shackles [hamstringing], for they made no attempt to seize estates. If sometimes the battle were more heated, they went so far as to burn towns and
devastate fields, but as soon as they had inflicted the desired damage, they
regathered in their own lands without attempting to take possession of the
lands of others.

Other evidence does not support this view.

Garcilaso believed that the natives' enmity and hatred sprang primarily from a desire to demonstrate their valor and strength of spirit and
to gain experience in military science (Varner and Varner 1951:488).
Apparently, he believed that since the Mississippians did not engage in
pitched battles in the open or occupy land in the sense of the European
or Inkan political systems with which he was familiar, they did not control or dominate subject populations and their resources. He thought
the Mississippian military strategy could best be described as ambush
warfare rather than conquest warfare—in spite of his own descriptions
of well-orchestrated attacks both on land against stockaded towns and
on water in flotillas of 200–250 canoes with forty to eighty persons
per canoe. Garcilaso or his informants did not recognize the hegemonic
nature of the political system: once force had been applied with deadly
efficiency and ruthlessness, the threat of force was often sufficient to
keep a vassal or vassals in line (Dye 1990). In a political environment
based on perceived power and the threat of military force, a standing
army was not necessary to maintain authority over one's vassals.

Ambush warfare was an integral component of sixteenth-century
warfare. It was an intelligence-gathering mechanism that provided
means of assessing one's enemies' relative strengths and weaknesses and
of collecting information from captives. Small warrior contingents may
have afforded more personal freedom in the pursuit of victims, therefore allowing individuals to gain greater personal prestige and honor
than they might have achieved under the command of a higher-ranking
warrior. Small group size, necessary for ambush warfare, may have
engendered an egalitarian atmosphere and may have been structured according to kin ties, particularly affinally related males within the same

matriclan. Where the pursuits of a hunting party ended and the endeavors of a small war party began would be difficult to ascertain. Anyone and everyone was the object of an ambush in an environment charged with smoldering emotional and physical hostility directed against neighboring polities. Ambush warfare was based on interpolity feuding often across and within mutually held buffer zones and may have provided a way to resolve conflicts and tensions within a village by turning intratown aggression toward an adjacent polity.

Garcilaso underscores the nature of continuous hostilities among Mississippi Valley polities, where the threat of violence was a day-to-day reality: "Regardless of where they are found, they always are provided with arms, for in no place are they secure from their enemies. And the circumstance of their being so practiced in continuous fighting gives rise to that of their being of such a bellicose nature and so skillful with their weapons, particularly with the bow and arrows, for these being shooting arms with which they can be effective from a distance, they, as hunters who go in search of both men and animals, use them to a greater extent than they do others" (Varner and Varner 1951:488). A noble's greatest adornment was his best bow and arrows (Varner and Varner 1951:490).

Less frequent but with greater and more far-reaching consequences for the ruling elite, who were engaged in intense interchiefdom rivalry, was conquest warfare, which was well documented by the Spaniards. Large, well-planned, coordinated attacks were infrequent but endemic to the central Mississippi Valley and Mississippian polities in general. The threat of attack—whether real, imagined, or contrived—against a town may have provided chiefs with some measure of authority and control. Moats and ditches to connect them with adjacent bodies of water had to be excavated. Timbers had to be cut and placed next to the moats as palisades. War canoes had to be constructed. Preparations for attack and chains of command had to be instituted and recognized. The level of organization of military operations, for either offensive or defensive posturing, required centralized management and control, which in turn provided opportunities for political growth and empowerment in both economic and ideological spheres.

Land-based aggression in Mississippi Valley chiefdoms was clearly an endeavor on the behalf of chiefs to extend their political power regionally through conquest warfare. Chiefdom-level warfare is often directed more toward controlling populations and their labor in order to extract tribute than at holding territory (Carneiro 1970, 1990; Helms 1979; Johnson and Earle 1987:210; Price 1984). Limitations of culti-vatable soils by swamps, upland habitats, and lakes and rivers effec-tively limited the options of escape for conquered populations (Carneiro 1970). Thus, sixteenth-century Mississippians defended themselves in nucleated settlements fortified by ditches, embankments, and palisades. When the town did not provide sufficient protection, the inhabitants re-treated to remote or inaccessible areas or scattered out from the town into the "wilderness." [16] In fact, canoes were maintained in a state of readiness in the event the inhabitants were forced to flee their town (Varner and Varner 1951:487).

The nature of military strategy in chiefly warfare is not well under-stood; the Maori, for example, enlisted a variety of tactics (Vayda 1956:30–35). Native Americans in eastern North America in the seven-teenth and eighteenth centuries often tried to draw the enemy into traps through feints or mock retreats. In the sixteenth century, as native groups came into contact with large contingents of Europeans, town aban-donment was a favored tactic throughout the Southeast. Coordinated movements of groups of warriors on land and water appear to have been commonplace in the Southeast but fell into disuse by the beginning of the eighteenth century. A variety of strategies probably were used both by defenders of fortified towns and by those attempting to gain access to the towns.

Lacustrine or riverine warfare was an important component of chiefly conquest in the central Mississippi Valley. Canoes were plentiful on the Mississippi during the mid-sixteenth century, and paramount chiefs, who controlled 200 to 250 war canoes, were capable of sophisticated tactics, including enfilade, in addition to transporting military forces and interdicting river traffic (Lafferty 1977), which in turn allowed them to control the goods trade and the movement of people across the land-scape. The ability to transport large numbers of military personnel along the Mississippi and through the interfluvial waterways may have been the backbone of the hegemonic system, granting a chief control over a larger amount of land than could otherwise be achieved by ground forces. The central Mississippi Valley inhabitants in the mid-sixteenth century believed themselves to be more powerful against the Spaniards on water than on land (Varner and Varner 1951:564), in part because the conquerors could not use their horses, dogs, or heavy European armor and weapons—such as muskets, swords, pikes, halberds, and cross-bows—in boats. Another interpretation is that the Mississippians felt superior to the Spaniards simply because they were more accustomed to fighting in that environment.[17] Also, they may have witnessed or been informed of the entrada's efforts to cross the Mississippi on June 18, 1541, which probably appeared as an amateurish maneuver to a people adept at aquatic transportation.

As was the case in Panamanian chiefdoms, warfare was oriented toward the destruction of elite dwellings, especially sacred buildings containing the remains of the honored dead and their associated *sacra*. Mississippian towns, like their Panamanian counterparts, "stood forth as overt evidence of high status and authority, prestige and power of the ruler" (Helms 1979:9), and their destruction was essential to remove the existing elite's access to power and ultimately usurp their links to sources of power such as nodes on trade networks, supernatural forces, and military activities.

Chiefs raised battalions of warriors numbering in the thousands who were trained to travel and fight as coordinated units on land and water. Warriors who participated in these maneuvers may have been ranked. For example, Natchez warriors were divided into three classes: true warriors, ordinary warriors, and apprentice warriors (Tregle 1975:371). Supplies for military contingents were carried by armed bearers. Chiefs directed and coordinated human labor and the political, economic, and ideological energy necessary to construct fortifications (palisades, bastions, and moats) and war canoes. The ultimate basis of Mississippian military organization in the central Mississippi Valley may have relied more on a chief's ability to coerce his supporters and followers than on his ability to build a faithful and devoted following through consensus.

Towns were destroyed and temples desecrated, houses looted, elite residences burned, and horticultural fields devastated. Subterfuges apparently were employed by occupants of fortified Mississippian towns to counterattack their assailants. If they lost, the inhabitants were either freed, captured for enslavement, or decapitated or scalped and probably dismembered, and the various bodily parts displayed in public areas. The fact that so much was destroyed, including human life, underscores the idea that warfare "at the chiefdom level often did more to increase the power and status of the paramount chief than it did to enlarge his domain" (Carneiro 1990:207). In this regard warfare in the central Mississippi Valley resembled warfare programs of complex chiefdoms in other parts of the world such as Panama (Helms 1979), the Cauca Valley of Colombia, Polynesia (Carneiro 1990), and New Zealand (Vayda 1956).

NOTES

I wish to thank John H. House, Charles Hudson, Robert H. Lafferty III, and Jeffrey M. Mitchem for their comments on an earlier draft of this paper. Appreciation is also expressed to Patricia B. Kwachka and Jerald T. Milanich for their invitation to participate in the symposium "The Southeast at the Time of Columbus" and for their editorial comments. Mary W. Helms also provided editorial advice. To all the above I am appreciative, but I assume responsibility for any errors contained herein.

1. An alternative interpretation of the ethnohistoric and archaeological data suggests that the de Soto expedition crossed the Mississippi River near Clarksdale, Mississippi (Atkinson 1987; Brain 1984, 1985a; Brain et al. 1974; Swanton 1939; Weinstein 1985, 1992).

2. A great deal of discussion has been generated concerning the relative merits of the four primary accounts of the de Soto expedition (see Anderson 1990:95–99; Brain et al. 1974; Galloway 1991; Henige 1986; Hudson et al. 1989; Phillips et al. 1951; Swanton 1932, 1939). Most scholars would agree that Rangel's account is the most trustworthy of the four and that Garcilaso's version is the least reliable. Hernández de Biedma and Elvas fall in between, with the former perhaps enjoying somewhat more credibility than the latter.

3. Quizquiz maintained a continuous state of war with the Chickasaw (Varner and Varner 1951:423); Casqui and Pacaha had waged intense war against one another for a long time (Elvas 1922:119; Hernández de Biedma 1922:26, 30; Rangel 1922:139; Varner and Varner 1951:434); Guachoya and Nilco were at war with each other (Elvas 1922:150; Hernández de Biedma 1922:34; Varner and Varner 1951:487); Nilco was at war with Aminoya (Elvas 1922:185); and Guachoya was at war with Quigualtam (Elvas 1922:195, 197). Polities not mentioned as being in a state of war may have been part of an alliance or may have been held as vassals, as was the case with Quizquiz and possibly Aquixo to Pacaha (Hernández de Biedma 1922:25) and Guachoya to Nilco (Varner and Varner 1951:492).

4. These ditches, in addition to their defensive function, also served as safe harbors for canoes in time of rough water or attack (Lafferty 1986).

5. The unit of measure here appears to be wrong; a depth of ten to twelve

feet would be more reasonable. Excavations at the Parkin site reveal that the depth of the moat encircling the site was six and a quarter feet from the lowest point of the present ground surface, and the width was more than eighty-four feet (Jeffrey M. Mitchem 1991). This description of the Pacaha waterworks fits the description of several archaeological sites in the central Mississippi Valley.

6. The common league was approximately three and a half miles (Chardon 1980:302; Hudson et al. 1984:66).

7. If the war canoes could hold up to seventy-five warriors each, then Garcilaso's estimate of three thousand warriors seems appropriate.

8. Nilco's "captain general" reported the Nilco massacre to Gonzalo Silvestre (Varner and Varner 1951:546).

9. Garcilaso's figure of six thousand canoes may refer to the number of people involved in the crossing rather than the number of vessels. If that were the case, then his figure would agree with Rangel's estimate of seven thousand warriors.

10. If Aquixo was vassal to Pacaha (Hudson 1985:3; D. Morse 1991:46), then Elvas and Rangel would be in agreement.

11. The white plumes in the headdresses may have been swan (*Olor* sp.) or snow goose (*Chen caerulescens*) feathers. Both swan and snow goose wings were found with burials at Rhodes (3CT3), swan wings were found at Bradley (3CT7), and a snow goose wing was recovered from Pecan Point (3MS78) (Moore 1911:414–16, 430, 452). Paul Parmalee (1966:144) and Gregory Perino (1966:46) report both snow goose/blue goose and swan wings from Banks (3CT13). Chickasaw warriors wore swan feathers as part of their headgear (S. C. Williams 1973:173).

12. Hernández de Biedma supports Garcilaso's characterization of the number of men the vessels were capable of carrying: "The second day, descending the stream, there came out against us some forty or fifty very large and swift canoes, in some of which were as many as eighty warriors" (1922:39). While Garcilaso's estimates are often considered extreme, descriptions of Maori war canoes (Best 1925:25–119) and their striking resemblance to those used on the Mississippi suggest that Garcilaso's estimates are within the realm of possibility for chiefdoms: "On the average, the [war] canoes accommodated seventy people and were some seventy feet long. They were manned by a double row of warriors who plied their paddles in time to the chants and gestures of one or two leaders standing amidships" (Vayda 1956:25).

13. The description of Quigualtam's maneuvering on the Mississippi suggests that as the Spanish fleet moved downstream the Quiguaitam warriors took advantage of the current to maneuver their fleet along the western concave banks, then moved in front of the expedition in the reaches between the bends; then, holding along the eastern concave bank, they crossed behind the brigan-

tines in the next riffle area. The war canoes could cross in front of and behind the Spaniards in the reaches of the river where the centrifugal force was minimized, thus avoiding the centrifugal force along the concave banks of the river bends. The Spaniards themselves may have taken advantage of this principle of the river on the advice of the Quizquizians when they initially crossed the river on June 18, 1541 (Dye 1992).

14. A crossbow shot is about 300 yards, or 273 meters (Hudson 1990:38; Swanton 1939:108).

15. This chiefdom may represent the protohistoric Natchez, as eighteen days would place the expedition in the vicinity of Natchez, Mississippi.

16. Town abandonment had been the case with the Aminoya's two principle towns (Varner and Varner 1951:532), several Aquixo towns (Elvas 1922:117), the Coligoa town (Elvas 1922:133), the town of Guachoya (Elvas 1922:151), the main Pacahan town (Elvas 1922:124–25; Hernández de Biedma 1922:28; Varner and Varner 1951:437, 446), the town of Nilco (Varner and Varner 1951:532), a Palisema town (Elvas 1922:134), the main Quiguate town (Elvas 1922:130; Varner and Varner 1951:451), and another Quiguate town (Elvas 1922:131; see Dye 1990).

17. Thomas Holland (1991:219) notes that males from the Campbell site (23PM5) in southeastern Missouri "spent a great deal of time in the water."

Ethnic Identities and Cultural Change in the Protohistoric Period of Eastern Arkansas

Michael P. Hoffman

While the identification of ethnic groups in the late prehistoric and protohistoric periods in eastern Arkansas may seem like a hopelessly nineteenth-century goal long ago addressed by the likes of ethnologist John Swanton, the task has assumed a new timeliness because Public Law 101-601, the Native American Graves Protection and Repatriation Act, demands it of certain archaeological collections. Archaeologists, particularly those associated with museums, often *have* to make ethnic assessments of archaeological collections that include human remains and funerary objects so that descendant tribes can make repatriation decisions.

Furthermore, there are more data available today to help make ethnic identifications, particularly in archaeology and bioarchaeology, than in Swanton's day. Ethnohistory, historical linguistics, Native American mythology, and ethnology continue to provide useful sources of information.

This essay discusses the ethnic identifications of the period from about A.D. 1450 to 1700 in northeastern and east-central Arkansas. The issues of the antiquity of the Quapaw in the area and the possible identification of other tribes there are critical in determining the rightful owners of funerary and sacred objects liable for repatriation.

NORTHEASTERN AND EAST-CENTRAL ARKANSAS

The area involved is part of the lower Mississippi alluvial valley, which extends from Little Rock to Memphis and from the mouth of the

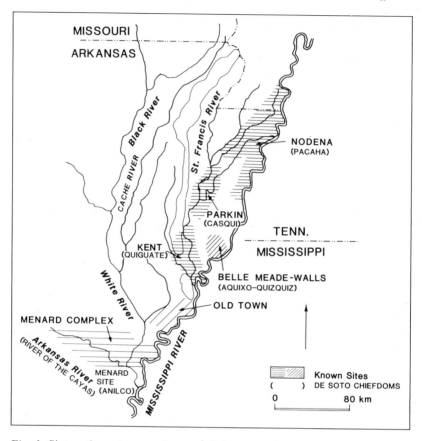

Fig. 1. Sixteenth-century northeastern Arkansas archaeological phases and town names from the de Soto narratives.

Arkansas River valley on the south to the Missouri bootheel on the north (Figure 1). A number of late Mississippian phases existed in northeastern Arkansas at least until the middle of the sixteenth century. These include the Nodena phase along the Mississippi River above Memphis to just above the Missouri line (D. Morse 1990), the Parkin phase along the Little and St. Francis rivers (P. Morse 1990), the Walls–Belle Meade phases around Memphis (G. Smith 1990), the Kent phase of the lower St. Francis River drainage (House 1987), and the little-known Old Town phase on the Mississippi River below the mouth of the St. Francis River (D. Morse and Morse 1983:297–98).

In east-central Arkansas there is an archaeological manifestation called the Menard Complex, a term recently revived to replace the misleading term "Quapaw phase" formerly in use (D. Morse 1991). The Menard Complex, which dates to perhaps A.D. 1450–1700, extends along the lower Arkansas River from above Little Rock to the vicinity of the mouths of the Arkansas and White rivers.

These archaeological manifestations belong to the general late Mississippian culture and show substantial maize agriculture, town-mound centers, wattle-and-daub structures, and shell-tempered pottery of diverse shapes and decorations. Northeastern Arkansas settlement was nucleated in the town-mound centers, but the pattern along the lower Arkansas River is still poorly understood.

The Nodena and Parkin phases, and probably the rest of the archaeological manifestations discussed in this essay, crystallized in the latter part of the fourteenth century at about the time the Cairo Lowland region to the north was beginning to be abandoned. Dan and Phyllis Morse (1983:282–83) consider it likely that people from the north were absorbed into these Arkansas phases.

DE SOTO–ERA CHIEFDOMS AND ARCHAEOLOGICAL PHASES

Archaeologists in Arkansas currently believe that the northern de Soto expedition route in 1541–43 postulated by Morse and Morse (1983) and Charles Hudson (1985) fits the archaeological, linguistic, geographical, and ethnological information better than the more southern routes favored by John Swanton (1939) and Jeffrey Brain (1985b). If that is the case, the following correlations can be made: the Nodena phase and the chiefdom of Pacaha; the Parkin phase and the chiefdom of Casqui; the Walls–Belle Meade phases and the chiefdoms of Quizquiz-Aquixo; and the Kent phase and the chiefdom of Quiguate. The "River of the Cayas" in the de Soto narratives is the Arkansas River. On that stream, Anilco, near the river's mouth, is the Menard site of the Menard Complex. Much further upstream in central Arkansas, Tanico is identified with the Carden Bottoms phase (Hoffman 1990).

The accounts of the de Soto expedition in northeastern Arkansas depict complex chiefdoms with fortified nucleated town centers. Cultivated maize provided the bulk of the food, and warfare was very important.

LATE SEVENTEENTH-CENTURY FRENCH ACCOUNTS
OF ETHNIC GROUPS

There is a 130-year gap between the last de Soto expedition and the 1673 voyage down the Mississippi River by Marquette and Jolliet. During this hiatus major changes must have occurred in northeastern and east-central Arkansas because the French encountered no Indian communities in northeastern Arkansas. On the Mississippi River they saw no Indian villages until they came across the villages of the Quapaw tribe a short distance above the mouth of the White and Arkansas rivers. Marquette and Jolliet were told through their Illinois interpreters that a village of the Mitchigamea Illinois existed in northeastern Arkansas and that at least five Indian villages were present west of the Quapaw (Akansea) villages on what is usually interpreted as the lower Arkansas River. By A.D. 1700 only the three or four Quapaw villages near the mouth of the Arkansas River still remained in northeastern and east-central Arkansas.

The ethnic identity of the Indians on the lower Arkansas River in east-central Arkansas in the late seventeenth century is clearer as a result of Robert Rankin's (1988a) linguistic analysis of place-names on the 1673 Marquette map (Figure 2). The Dhegiha Siouan Quapaw (Akansea) lived on the banks of the Mississippi River near the mouth of the White and Arkansas rivers, and some distance up the Arkansas River were towns linked to Tunican speakers (Tanik8a, Papikaha, Mem8eta) and the linguistically related Koroans (Akoroa, Matora; see Rankin 1988a:11–12). Thus the linguistic data indicate that the Quapaws were present on the Mississippi River near the mouth of the White and Arkansas rivers and Tunican-related peoples were present on the lower Arkansas River in the late seventeenth century.

EAST-CENTRAL ARKANSAS ARCHAEOLOGICAL
MANIFESTATIONS IN THE SEVENTEENTH CENTURY

Until very recently all of the late prehistoric–protohistoric archaeological remains found along the lower Arkansas River were grouped into a single Quapaw phase, with the implication that these represented the Quapaw tribe (Ford 1961; Phillips 1970; Hoffman 1977, 1986); but

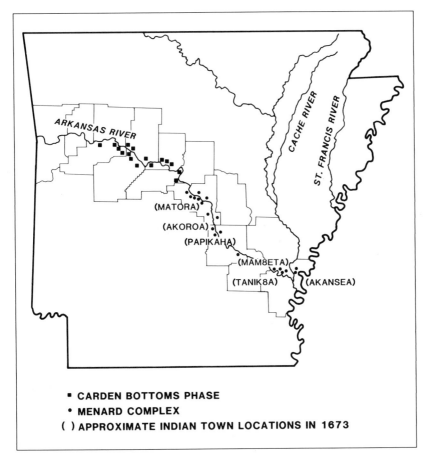

• CARDEN BOTTOMS PHASE
• MENARD COMPLEX
( ) APPROXIMATE INDIAN TOWN LOCATIONS IN 1673

Fig. 2. Protohistoric archaeological manifestations along the central and lower Arkansas River and approximate locations of Indian towns on the Marquette 1673 map.

there were problems with this facile correlation. One problem, popularly referred to as "the Quapaw paradox," was that the ceramics of the phase reveal strong ties to native eastern Arkansas late Mississippian cultures, while Quapaw tribal traditions and linguistic and ethnological ties indicate strong links with other Dhegiha Siouan tribes outside the lower Mississippi Valley. The four Quapaw villages described in the late seventeenth century by the French (which were on the Mississippi River or a very short distance upstream from the mouth of the Arkansas River) do not seem similar to the many protohistoric Quapaw phase

sites distributed along the Arkansas River up to the vicinity of Little
Rock. A second problem was that no evidence of the Quapaws' distinctive long, bark-covered houses was found in the excavations of Quapaw
phase sites.

Because of these inconsistencies as well as other doubts, Arkansas
archaeologists who work in the region today have abandoned the term
"Quapaw phase" in favor of the more neutral "Menard Complex" to
describe the protohistoric remains along the lower Arkansas River.

The ceramics from several sites of the Menard Complex show some
similarities to those defined as characteristic of the historic Tunica in
Mississippi and Louisiana by Brain (1988), including widespread occurrence of Brain's "Tunica mode" and incised pottery similar to the Tunican signature type, Winterville Incised, variety *Tunica*. There are also
pottery shapes and designs in this and other protohistoric Arkansas River
sites that are *not* part of Brain's Tunica ceramic complex. These may
reflect indigenous Arkansas River developments and trade with adjacent
peoples.

HISTORIC ETHNIC AND LINGUISTIC GROUPS
IN EAST-CENTRAL ARKANSAS

Tunica

Tunican and Quapaw peoples lived in east-central Arkansas in the
latter half of the seventeenth century, but how are these groups related
to the people who lived there in the sixteenth and fifteenth centuries?
There is fairly good evidence that the Tunica dominated the late prehistoric and early protohistoric periods and that the Quapaw did not enter
the scene until the middle to late seventeenth century.

The language, lifeways, and history of the Tunica have been the subjects of much research in this century (Swanton 1911; Haas 1950, 1953;
Brain 1979, 1988, 1990). Jeffrey Brain, an archaeologist and ethno-
historian from the Peabody Museum at Harvard University, has been
able to trace the tribe's presence archaeologically and historically from
its current location at Marksville on the Red River in Louisiana back to
locations near the mouth of the Red River in Louisiana and the mouth of
the Yazoo River, where the tribe had moved by 1699 (Brain 1979, 1988,

1990). Especially at the Trudeau site near the mouth of the Red River in Louisiana, which was occupied between A.D. 1731 and 1764, native-manufactured ceramics and other artifacts established the archaeological complex characteristic of the tribe.

Brain is not able to document the Tunica prior to 1699 with as much certainty. Before the protohistoric "dark ages" between 1543 and 1673 he identifies the Tunica with the western Mississippi de Soto–era entity of Quizquiz, which he locates on the Sunflower River drainage near Clarksdale, Mississippi (Brain 1988). Rather than using ceramic continuity as a basis for linking earlier Tunica sites, Brain uses ethnohistoric data for this identification. First, both the historic Tunica and the denizens of Quizquiz had agricultural fields worked by men, an unusual feature in the Southeast. Second, Tunican traditions recount that they once lived farther north, along the Mississippi River above the mouth of the Yazoo River (Brain 1990). Finally, Choctaw and Chickasaw peoples referred to Mississippian culture archaeological sites near Clarksdale as "Tunica Oldfields." Consequently, Brain favors a southern route for the crossing of the Mississippi River by the de Soto expedition and so identifies the Mississippi archaeological phases of Huspuckena II and Parchman with the chiefdom of Quizquiz (1988:272). (Those who favor the Morse-Hudson northern route identify the Walls phase with Quizquiz.)

There are indications that Tunican speakers dominated east-central and northeastern Arkansas in the 1540s. The chiefdom of Cayas-Tanico, which Hudson (1985) locates at Carden Bottoms in the central Arkansas River valley, is widely accepted as Tunican because Tanico is one of the alternative spellings Europeans commonly used for people who spoke the distinctive Tunican languages (Jetcr 1986). Further linguistic evidence from the de Soto narratives links the northeastern Arkansas chiefdom of Pacaha with the Tunican language. John Swanton (1939) postulated, and Robert Rankin recently confirmed with modern analysis, that three native words recorded at Pacaha—*mochila, macanoche,* and *caloosa*—reflect Tunican phonology, phonetics, and semantics when compared with Mary Haas's (1953) Tunica dictionary (Rankin 1988a: 7–8). Rankin also postulates a linguistic link between Pacaha and the late seventeenth-century lower Arkansas River Indian town name of Papikaha (1988a:11), and he suggests population movement from northeastern Arkansas to the Arkansas River valley between the late sixteenth and the late seventeenth centuries. Based on linguistic and cultural evidence from the de Soto narratives, George Sabo (1992:19) speculates that the central Mississippi Valley area in Arkansas from Pacaha in extreme northeastern Arkansas to Anilco and Autiamque on the lower Arkansas River was inhabited by people who spoke a Tunican language. The late prehistoric and early protohistoric archaeological manifestations of the northeastern Arkansas area dominated by Tunica in the sixteenth century are relatively homogeneous in settlement and subsistence; their ceramics differ in minor ways. The Walls phase of the Memphis locality—Quizquiz according to the northern de Soto route postulated by Morse and Hudson—also conforms. This high degree of similarity in sixteenth-century northeastern Arkansas sites has prompted Stephen Williams to postulate a single terminal Mississippian phase for the area representing a "washing over" of earlier phase differences, the Armorel phase (1980:105).

Koroa

The Koroa group of Tunican speakers was also present in seventeenth-century eastern Arkansas. This little-known group was closely associated with both the Tunica and the Natchez during the seventeenth and early eighteenth centuries (Swanton 1911:331–32) and, after suffering greatly during the French wars with the Natchez, was absorbed by the Chickasaw or Choctaw by the middle 1700s. The 1673 Marquette map places villages called Akoroa and Matora on the lower Arkansas River (Rankin 1988a:15). A seventeenth-century indication of Koroan presence in southeastern Arkansas comes from Henri de Tonti, who twice visited villages there (Dickinson 1980). The linguistic case for sixteenth-century Koroans in northeastern Arkansas is not as strong as the general Tunican one. Swanton (1939) associates Coligua, a town name from the de Soto narratives, with Koroans. Rankin (1988a:15) finds phonetic difficulties with the association, although he still considers it a "strong possibility." Morse and Morse (1983) identify the Greenbriar phase on the White River near the edge of the Ozark Highlands as Coligua.

Kaskinampo

An interesting issue is the ethnic identity of the northeastern Arkansas sixteenth-century town of Casqui. Swanton (1939:52) ties this name to

Kaskinampo, a little-known Muskogean-speaking group from eastern Tennessee thought to be ancestral to the Koasati. According to Rankin (1988a:5), *casqui* means 'warrior' in Koasati, but he is skeptical of the Casqui-Kaskinampo link because the Kaskinampo people known to history were so geographically distant (1988a:5). Nor were there any other nearby Muskogean-speaking peoples. Sabo (1992) does not perceive strong cultural boundaries between Pacaha and Casqui based on the de Soto narratives. According to the northern de Soto route scenario (Morse and Morse 1983), Casqui is Parkin phase, a unit not distinctly different from other contemporary northeastern Arkansas archaeological manifestations.

Quapaw

The date of the Quapaw tribe's first presence in Arkansas is an important issue. The historic tribe is linguistically and ethnologically distinct from other lower Mississippi Valley peoples. A tribal tradition recounts a recent movement to Arkansas in which the Quapaw drove out the Tunica and Illini (Bizzell 1981). Tunican oral tradition says that they were forced by newcomers to leave an earlier location along the Mississippi (Brain 1990:13).

Marquette and Jolliet encountered the Quapaw in 1673 in a limited area on the Mississippi River near the mouths of the White and Arkansas rivers. They were told that there were only four villages in this small area. Marquette's map indicates Tunican villages only on the lower Arkansas River.

There is no ethnological or linguistic evidence in the de Soto narratives for a sixteenth-century Quapaw presence in Arkansas. No descriptions of the distinctive Quapaw houses exist in the narratives. Robert Rankin, a linguist whose specialty is Dhegiha Siouan, states that "as things stand now it does not appear that De Soto encountered any Siouan speaking peoples on his trek through Arkansas, or through the Southeast, for that matter, outside of Catawba" (1988a:17). He rejects the Garcilaso version of Pacaha as Capaha cited by those who favor a Quapaw presence in sixteenth-century northeastern Arkansas (D. Morse 1991) because all three firsthand accounts use "Pacaha" (Rankin 1988a:7). Also, two terms cited in the narratives from Pacaha, *macanoche* and *mochila,* could not have been in the Quapaw language, which lacked the *chuh* sound (Rankin 1988a:9). Both terms are based on Tunican sounds and meanings.

Archaeological remains of the historical Quapaw tribe have not been unambiguously identified. It is now apparent that many of the remains thought by James A. Ford (1961) to be Quapaw actually represent Arkansas River Tunica. A direct historical approach to identify Quapaw archaeological remains is possible in east-central Arkansas and might clear up the confusion. Since that tribe was the only one that remained there in the eighteenth century, historical documents and ground surveys could be used to find and excavate a village of that time. Then an unambiguous archaeological complex for the Quapaw could be identified and followed backward in time to trace the tribe's history in Arkansas. At present I see no strong evidence for a Quapaw presence in Arkansas in the sixteenth century, and there is historical evidence for their presence by the last quarter of the seventeenth century only in a tiny cluster of villages at the mouth of the Arkansas and White rivers. Their own accounts of their recent movement to Arkansas and conflicts with the Tunica should be taken seriously.

Contrary to the prevailing view only a few years ago, it is likely that Tunican-speaking people are responsible for most of the cultural remains in northeastern and east-central Arkansas in the A.D. 1400–1700 period. With the possible exception of the Kaskinampo (Parkin phase), they were the people visited and described by the mid-sixteenth-century de Soto expeditions in both regions. When northeastern Arkansas was abandoned toward the end of the sixteenth century, the Tunican peoples joined their kinsmen along the central and lower Arkansas River. By the end of that century the intrusive Quapaw had driven them out of Arkansas into western Mississippi and northeastern Louisiana.

Of course there are problems in this interpretation. A major weakness is that no specific archaeological complex has been proposed for the historic Quapaw. Also, evidence that verifies the Quapaws' location before they came to Arkansas is lacking (the lower Ohio Valley or southern Illinois and adjacent Missouri are sometimes postulated). These issues need to be addressed in future research projects.

Making the Connection: Is It Possible to Link the Koasati to an Archaeological Culture?

Geoffrey Kimball

The identification of an archaeological culture with an ethnographic one is a topic that has tantalized American archaeology for years. I intend to use linguistic and archaeological information as well as ethnohistorical and ethnographic material to test the possibility that the Koasati Indians presently residing in Louisiana come from the archaeological culture known as the Dallas phase or focus.

ETHNOHISTORICAL BACKGROUND

Seventeenth-century maps occasionally call the Tennessee River the "Coasatees River" (Moll 1711). The following is a description of the Tennessee River from that period: "The most Southerly of the above-said four Rivers, which enter into the Lake, is a River some call *Kasqui*, so nam'd from a Nation Inhabiting a little above its Mouth; others call it the *Cusates* or the River of the *Cheraquees* a mighty Nation, among whom it hath its chief Fountains. . . . Thirty or fourty leagues above the *Chicazas*, this River forms four delicate Islands which have each a Nation Inhabiting them, *viz. Tahogale, Kakigue, Cochali*, and *Tali*" (French 1741:13–14). By 1730 the Koasati were settled below the confluence of the Coosa and Talapoosa rivers in Alabama, near Fort Toulouse (D'Anville 1752). In 1795 the Koasati moved from Alabama to Spanish Louisiana, and soon after the Louisiana Purchase they moved to Spanish Texas. From the 1830s to the 1870s they filtered back into southwestern Louisiana; they established their present settlement north of Elton, Louisiana, in 1882.

By the time travelers began to record features of their material and social culture in the early nineteenth century, Koasati society had changed drastically from its original form. Wealth was now gauged by the ownership of horses, cattle, and hogs; fruit trees of European origin were planted in their gardens; and visitors were served thick black coffee (as they are to this day). Aboriginal technology was supplanted to a great degree by European technology; thus the Koasatis' material culture, so important in the archaeological record, was already greatly altered from their Mississippian origins.

ARCHAEOLOGICAL BACKGROUND

Because the earliest records place the Koasati in eastern Tennessee, and the Dallas component is the latest Mississippian culture found in that area, the Koasati have been tentatively equated with the Dallas component (T. Lewis and Kneberg 1946). The Mouse Creek focus, contemporaneous to and geographically adjacent to the Dallas focus, has been identified as the Yuchi by Theodore Lewis and Madeline Kneberg. They also suggest intermarriage of Mouse Creek into Dallas on the basis of variance in burial customs among the Dallas occupants of Hiwassee Island. Linguistic evidence suggests that this analysis is correct, for there are a number of words that indicate contact between the Koasati and the Yuchi (Ballard 1973):

Koasati	Yuchi	English
čissí	*čʰisane*	'mouse'
čokko	*cuk?o*	'muscadine'/'poison sumac'
histó	*west*	'ashes'
imiyatí:ka	*yatik'e*	'interpreter'; cf. Creek *yatika*
lopí	*?yΛpi*	'liver'
łahi	*ła?i*	'shoot and hit'
łakí	*ła*	'arrow'
sattá	*c'Λtʰa*	'turtle'
tała	*doła*	'weave'

Yuchi is a language isolate that may be distantly related to the Siouan family. The Koasati and Yuchi peoples have not been in contact at any time during the historic period, so it is not possible that these words were borrowed later.

There are fewer words that indicate Koasati contact with the Cherokee. The majority are natural history terms, many of which seem to have an areal spread, such as the terms for 'robin' and 'buffalo':

Koasati	Cherokee	English	Notes
čiskoko	ci:sk^wok^wo	'robin'	cf. Choctaw *biskoko;* Tuscarora *cisku?u;* Tunica *wísk?ohku*
čokbila:bila	ck^walek^wala	'whippoorwill'	
čola	cula	'fox'	cf. Creek *čola;* Choctaw *čola*
hanono	kanuna	'bullfrog'	
kowassá:ti	akusa	'Koasati'/'Creek'	
nočilolo	no:ksi	'meadowlark'	cf. Creek *hanači:lo;* Choctaw *sọlolo*
yanasá	yansa	'buffalo'	cf. Creek *yanasa;* Choctaw *yanaš*

Siouan languages were apparently spoken to the north and west. There are a few items indicating contact; the most important is the numeral suffix -*nannan* 'in groups of *N*'. This is derived from a form like Quapaw -*nạnạ*. The word for 'nine' has been borrowed widely in the Southeast, so it is possible to have "cognate" forms in unrelated languages; for example, Koasati: *čakká:linánnan;* Quapaw: *šakkanạnạ;* English: 'in groups of nine'.

Other forms showing similarity are natural history terms, which may be areal in nature; for example, Koasati: *tiskommá* (*hómma* 'red'); Ofo: *deska acuti* (*deska* 'bird', *acuti* 'red'); English: 'cardinal'; and the words for *woodpecker:* Koasati: *bakbá;* Quapaw: *poxpa;* and Catawba: *pakpi.*

LINGUISTIC TERMS AND THE ARCHAEOLOGICAL RECORD

The following discussion centers on Koasati linguistic terms for items that can be found archaeologically. There are about two dozen terms that pertain to aboriginal architecture. The basic terms are as follows:

albiná	'camp'
ó:la	'town'
ó:la imatanatlí	'city wall'; cf. *atanátkan* 'to encircle'
alholihtá	'enclosing wall'; cf. *holihtá* 'fence'
í:sa	'house'
stapahča	'arbor'

The terms for 'city wall' and 'enclosing wall' are now obsolete, but they clearly are applicable to the palisades that surrounded major Dallas sites. The term for 'house', literally meaning 'dwelling place', can refer to any building. The arbor was a roofed but unwalled structure used for sleeping and cooking in hot weather; it seems to have been similar to the Seminole chickee. The following are terms for areas and buildings within a town:

itbítka	'dancing ground'
ittó:ka	'ball ground'
kohtá	'ball pole'
iscobá	'church'

The word for 'church' apparently meant 'ritual building'. It could well have referred to the building or buildings that were built on mounds in Dallas sites. The dancing ground or ball ground would be equivalent to the plazas of archaeological sites. The presence of post holes at the ends of a plaza would indicate a ball ground.

In addition to the principal structures, there were structures classified by their building materials:

hałbí stí:sa	'bark house'
iłaní stí:sa	'cane house'
tá:la stí:sa	'palmetto house'
ittohísi stí:sa	'brush shelter'

The bark house at present is considered by elders to be the most ancient kind of building. It was constructed by sewing strips of pine bark to a framework of logs. On the other hand, the cane house, which within memory was used only for temporary shelters in camps, seems to be the more ancient form of construction. It was built by weaving canes among a framework of poles. This is identical with building construction during the Dallas phase, the only difference being that Koasati cane houses were not plastered. The palmetto house is a structure indigenous to the Indian tribes of Louisiana, from whom the Koasati adopted it. It was never used very frequently. The brush shelter was a crude construction of branches and leaves used for overnight shelter by hunters.

The Koasati built a few structures outside the town: *palpiyá:ka* 'bridge', *filbacá* 'foot-log'. The foot-log was an ad hoc solution to the problem of crossing a stream, but the bridge was a more permanent structure, and it is possible that traces of these remain.

Although building materials and techniques have changed radically over time (the oldest consultants recall the log cabin as being the standard form of house), the terms used to describe traditional building practices are still recalled:

čakpá	'four walls of a house'; 'four sides of a basket'
ittobakná	'log post'
ittofalaktó	'forked post used in house construction'
hałbí	'pin bark'
po:loslin	'to chink something'
okhayi:kací	'daub pit'
okhayi:lí:cin	'to make daub'

The most interesting term on this list is *cakpa* 'the four walls of a house; the four sides of a basket'. The Koasati do not have a word for 'wall' as it is understood in English meaning a single wall; for them the walls of a house are a unit. This concept is derived directly from Dallas building practices. A reconstruction of a Dallas building demonstrates that the walls form a single unit. Furthermore, the connection with sides of a basket is apropos considering that the most common kind of Koasati basket is four-sided, rectangular, and woven of cane, and the archaeological structures are four-sided, rectangular, and woven with cane.

Terms for stone-working technology also occur in Koasati. There is an elaboration of verbs describing the chipping of stone, which is appropriate for a society in which many major implements were made of stone.

acokná	'pick'
aksalí	'knife'
cá:fi	'axe'
łakí	'arrow'
ibi:acosó:ka	'arrowhead'
ibi:acóska	'arrowheads'
nisáffin	'to pressure-flake something (once)'
nislí:cin	'to pressure-flake something (twice or more)'
lofáplin	'to chip something lengthwise (once)'
loffí:cin	'to chip something (twice or more)'
łicóffin	'to chip something once by dropping it'
łicó:lin	'to chip something twice or more by dropping it'
sikáhlin	'to be chipped'

Chipped glass and stone arrowheads were produced as curiosities until 1992, when the last person who knew the techniques died. He only used pressure-flaking techniques and used the verbs *nisáffin* / *nislí:cin* to describe his work. He never had the occasion (or sufficiently large cores) to produce blades, but he knew the terms to describe their production. He did his pressure-flaking on his thigh, using deerskin as a guard and antler for the flaking tool. It is of interest that antler flakers are found in Dallas archaeological contexts.

Although pottery is the staple of archaeology, Koasati terms for pottery forms are few. One family still makes unglazed pottery to sell to collectors, but since they do not like being observed it is not clear if their techniques are aboriginal. The following are the Koasati pottery terms:

aykačí	'pot'
aykačabonohká	'drum'
čokbá	'narrow-necked vessel'
palá:na	'plate'

The one term of interest is that for 'drum'. Koasati drums were made by stretching a hide over the neck of a pottery vessel and binding it into place. The fact that pottery drums existed among the Koasati indicates their possible presence in the ancestral culture. It is possible that a Dallas plain jar with lugs, such as the one illustrated in plate 63D of Lewis and Kneberg (1946), could be a drum.

Terms for items made of bone and shell are few. One of interest is the word for 'spoon', since it is clearly related to the word for 'clam', and clamshell spoons occur in Dallas contexts. Another is 'nose ring', an item that should be recovered among grave articles.

cofá	'needle' (formerly 'awl')
copí	'beads'
foló	'spoon'; cf. *kayyaffoló* 'clam'
hakčotakká	'earrings'
ibisa:nataká:ka	'nose ring'
solohkací	'terrapin-shell rattles'

Metal technology is mentioned only for completeness. Even in recent times the Koasati have not been metalworkers. The only kind of metalworking they knew was cold-hammering. Older people remember that their elders used to cold-hammer silver coins into broaches, rings, and bracelets, and they recall two relevant terms: *oconá* 'metal', *lískan* 'to cold-hammer metal'. The only metal recovered from Dallas sites is sheet copper, which was probably made by cold-hammering.

PLACE-NAMES RECORDED BY DE SOTO AND PARDO

Place-names recorded by Hernándo de Soto and Juan Pardo have been used, quite rightly, to suggest the presence of Muskogean-language speakers in eastern Tennessee; however, not enough allowance is made for confusion of true names of towns with vocabulary items that the Spaniards took to be the names of towns or peoples. For example, Charles Hudson (1987) suggests that Pardo's "Casqui" is a corruption of the known town name Coste. In Koasati, however, the old word *kaskí* means 'warrior'; from the context, Pardo and his men are being warned of warriors coming from the various towns. Here a vocabulary term has been interpreted as a town name.

Spanish place-name	Koasati	English
Chiaha	*(ihá:ni) cayha*	'high (land)'
Olamico	*ó:la mikkó*	'chief town'
Chalahume	*okkali hó:mi*	'bitter spring'
Satap	*sinapo*	'ash tree'

A final note is called for concerning the equivalence of Koasati and Coste/Costehe. The variant Costehe can be resolved by the fact that place-names in Koasati are cited with the locative case suffix *-fa;* the fact that Koasati *f* is bilabial and not labiodental would lead it to be heard as *h;* misremembering would account for the vowel difference. Now what of Coste? There is a difficulty in equating it with *kowassá:ti,* for it requires that a long-accented syllable be syncoped in mispronunciation. This is not done in the later Spanish pronunciation Cosade or the English Coosada. My speculation is that Coste comes from *kowistílka* 'Panther-Clan Dwelling-Place'. According to tradition, Koasati clans (which include *kowí,* 'panther') were originally autonomous groups; the word *ayiksá* 'clan' also means 'tribe' or 'nation'. Thus the town of Coste (*kowistílka*)/Costehe (*kowistílkafa*) would then have been inhabited primarily by members of the Panther and related Wildcat (*kowaknasí*) clans.

What, then, does *kowassá:ti* mean? It could be merely a name. Many other southeastern tribal names cannot be interpreted—Choctaw, Chickasaw, Yuchi, and Mikasuki among them. But it seems to be at least partly analyzable: the element *-á:ti* seems to be equivalent to *át:i* 'human being'. We are then left with the element *kowass-;* the people of Kowass-. The lost final vowel can be *a* or *i,* *°kowassa* or *°kowassi.* The ethnohistorical evidence gathered by Hudson et al. (1987) indicates that the Dallas (Koasati) towns were under the political control of the chiefdom of Coosa. This suggests the possibility that Koasati means 'the people of Coosa', and that Kowassa was the name of the aboriginal chiefdom.

POINTS FOR ARCHAEOLOGISTS

The Koasati vocabulary terms suggest items of material culture that should be found in the archaeological record but are not yet attested.

Traces of minor buildings such as arbors should appear, and it may be possible to recover the traces of bridges if streambank erosion has not been extreme. Nose ornaments would be expected to occur in burial sites as a single ornament of bone or shell in front of the face of the deceased. Finally, Dallas pottery should be reevaluated with an eye toward recognizing the remains of pottery drums.

The interpretation of de Soto's and Pardo's place-names in some cases can be attested by archaeology. If Chalahume means 'bitter spring', is there a mineral spring near the site? These two cases offer a good opportunity to test the validity of interpretations of debatable place names.

This essay suggests that the Dallas component is the immediately prehistoric ancestor of the Koasati people. Although most of the evidence points to this conclusion, absolute certainty is not possible due to the lack of continuity between Dallas and modern Koasati material culture. Excavation of historic Koasati sites in Alabama, Texas, and Louisiana might provide the evidence necessary to prove or disprove this hypothesized relationship. So I end in uncertainty, where I began.

Where Did the Choctaw Come From? An Examination of Pottery in the Areas Adjacent to the Choctaw Homeland

Kenneth H. Carleton

At the time Hernando de Soto traveled through the Southeast, modern-day east-central Mississippi was unoccupied and had been unoccupied since the end of the late Woodland period (ca. A.D. 900–1000). No indisputably Mississippi period archaeological remains have ever been found there (Tesar 1974; Atkinson and Blakeman 1975; Atkinson 1976; Conn 1978; Penman 1980). Some artifacts have been attributed to the Mississippian, but these have all turned out to be eighteenth-century Choctaw instead. When the French first settled along the Gulf Coast in 1699, the Choctaw occupied a large area of present-day east-central and southeastern Mississippi and parts of west-central and southwestern Alabama. The obvious question is, where did the ancestors of the Choctaw come from?

THE CHOCTAW IN THE EIGHTEENTH CENTURY

Throughout the eighteenth century the Choctaw were divided into sociopolitical units called "divisions" or, later, "districts" by the Europeans who observed and wrote about them. It is not really clear from the historical documents how many divisions there were originally, or if there was even a fixed number; however, by the end of the eighteenth century there were primarily three divisions (Halbert 1901), each of which occupied, more or less, a single river drainage. The Eastern Division (the Ahepat Okla) occupied the western tributaries of the Tombigbee River in present-day Kemper and Lauderdale counties. The Western Division (the Okla Falaya) occupied the tributaries of the upper Pearl River in present-day Neshoba County and the Tallahatta and Chunky creeks area in the extreme northern drainage of the Chunky/Chikasawhay river system in present-day Newton County. The Southern, or Sixtowns, Division (the Okla Hannali) occupied the central and southern drainage of the Chunky/Chikasawhay system in present-day Newton, Jasper, and Clarke counties. Patricia Galloway (1994) interprets these divisions as the sociopolitical remnants of a late sixteenth- or seventeenth-century confederacy of refugee or remnant groups who came together (confederated) to form what we now know as the Choctaw. These groups came from one or more of the adjacent areas, from Mississippian populations disrupted by the introduction of European diseases, the natural cycle of chiefdom rise and fall, or both. The areas in which such Mississippian populations existed include (1) the lower Tombigbee/Mobile-Tensaw Delta and Mobile Bay region; (2) the central Tombigbee River drainage; (3) the upper Tombigbee River drainage/Black Prairie region (Oktibbeha, Clay, and Lowndes counties area); and (4) the central/lower Pearl River drainage.

If the constituent parts of the Choctaw came from one or more of these areas, there should be some similarities between the material culture of the eighteenth-century Choctaw and the late sixteenth- and/or seventeenth-century material cultures in these areas. In the case of ceramics, these similarities might include the temper used, vessel forms, either the decorative techniques or the motifs used, or any combination of these factors. In order to test this, sixteenth- and seventeenth-century ceramics from those adjacent areas were examined and compared with known eighteenth-century Choctaw ceramics to determine if any such similarities exist. Before I discuss the results of the comparison I should first give an overview of what is known about the eighteenth-century Choctaw ceramics.

EIGHTEENTH-CENTURY CHOCTAW CERAMICS

The current state of Choctaw ceramics classification is a confused hodgepodge of types and varieties based on results obtained by numerous researchers working with poor samples over the past sixty years (Collins 1927; Ford 1936:40–49; Haag 1953:25–28; Phillips 1970:65–66; Tesar 1974:114; Atkinson 1976:40; Atkinson and Blakeman 1975: 13–15; Penman 1980:285–86; Blitz 1985:81, 83; Voss and Blitz 1988; T. Mooney 1991: 89–94; Carleton 1992). The following discussion is a very general description of Choctaw ceramics based on their temper, decorative techniques and motifs, and their vessel forms, not an attempt to bring order to the confusion.

Based on their temper, Choctaw ceramics can be divided into the two broad categories of *Addis-like paste* and *coarse shell-tempered paste*. The first group can be further subdivided based on temper, decorative technique, and decorative motifs; the second needs no further subdivision for this discussion.

Addis Plain is a ceramic type originally described for the Natchez Bluffs area, and it occurs there in both prehistoric and historic contexts (Phillips 1970:48–49; S. Williams and Brain 1983:92; I. Brown 1985:288). It is a "heterogeneous paste containing inorganic and organic matter. [The] inorganic is largely grog, while [the] organic can consist of bone, charcoal, and even the occasional presence of shell" (I. Brown 1985:288). The primary Choctaw paste is similar enough to Addis to have been called that in the past, but in fact it varies from Addis in a number of ways, hence its designation here as "Addis-like." This variability primarily involves the tempering agents added to this "heterogeneous" mix.

There seems to have been a basic paste formula used by all the Choctaw to which other, variable tempering agents are added. These other agents vary from area to area within the Choctaw homeland. The basic paste formula includes clay and carbonized organics—perhaps ash, but this remains to be demonstrated. The variable agents include both inorganic substances and organics (Blitz 1985; Voss and Blitz 1988; Carleton 1992). Inorganics may be grog, claystone (a stone occurring naturally in east-central Mississippi predominantly made of compressed clay particles), and possibly sand. The organic agent is predominantly live shell. These agents appear to vary by division. Grog is common in the Eastern and Sixtowns divisions but has not been observed in the Western Division. Claystone is common in the Western Division but absent in the Sixtowns Division and is rare or absent in the Eastern Division. Shell is present in material from all three divisions but seems much more abundant in the Western Division ceramics. Unlike Addis, in which shell is only occasionally present, the Choctaw ceramics usually or often contain shell.

The decorative techniques used on the Addis-like Choctaw pottery can be divided into *incising* and *combing* (Figure 1). Combing uses an implement with multiple sharp teeth similar to a hair comb (they may actually have been broken trade combs; see Galloway 1984), which incises multiple lines simultaneously. Incising uses an implement with a single sharp point to incise individual lines, one at a time. The method of decoration seems to vary independently of the paste used to make the pottery (Voss and Blitz 1988:134); thus one can find either combed or incised sherds with grog (or any of the other variable agents) as temper. It is currently believed that combing was introduced later, after about 1750 (Galloway 1984; Voss and Blitz 1988:137). While recent discoveries I have made in Kemper County, Mississippi, tend to bear this out, this has not yet been definitely demonstrated.

The motifs used to decorate Choctaw pottery can be divided into three general categories: *geometric, rectilinear punctate,* and *curvilinear/rectilinear* (Figure 1). The most common geometric motifs are nested boxes, triangles (often depending from a single or double line along the vessel rim), line-filled triangles, and circles. Although both nested boxes and depended triangles have been observed as combed motifs, it is most common for these geometric motifs to be incised.

The rectilinear punctate motifs are composed of punctations, fingernail nicks, or pinching from which a single incised line depends. The punctations, nicks, and pinches are placed along the rim or on the exterior immediately below the rim of the vessel with the lines descending along the shoulder of the vessel at a diagonal from each punctation. This motif has been observed only in incising.

The curvilinear/rectilinear motifs most commonly associated with Choctaw pottery are often referred to as "Natchezan motifs" due to their similarity to motifs used by the historic Natchez and their antecedents in the lower Mississippi Valley. They appear as scrolls that often begin (or end) with a squared or boxed end. These are the most common combed motif, but they are also common in incised designs.

Their greater frequency in sites known to date to the first half of the eighteenth century and their decrease in frequency in late eighteenth- and early nineteenth-century sites makes it seem that the rectilinear

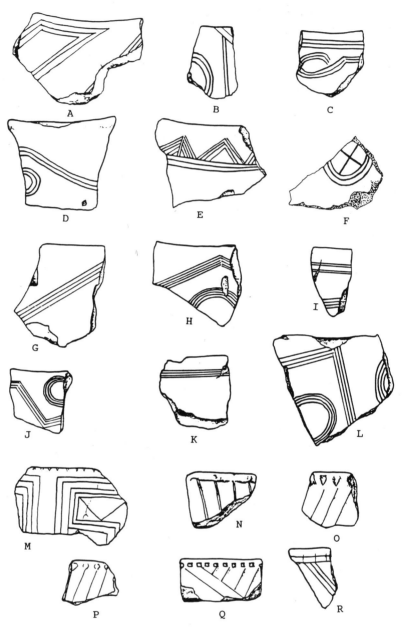

Fig. 1. Examples of eighteenth-century Choctaw ceramic motifs. A–D, curvi-
linear/rectilinear motifs; E–F, incised geometric motifs; G–L, combed curvi-
linear/rectilinear motifs; M–R, incised rectilinear punctate motifs (A–E and
G–R after Blitz 1985, figs. 4, 5, 7).

punctate motifs particularly, and the geometric motifs to some extent, are generally earlier than the curvilinear/rectilinear motifs. All these motifs have been observed in each of the divisions. The geometric and rectilinear punctate motifs are much more common in the Eastern and Sixtowns divisions than in the Western Division, although this may be a function of the age of the sites thus far located, with those in the Eastern and Sixtowns divisions representing earlier occupations than those in the Western Division.

The small size of the sherds typically recovered from most Choctaw sites has limited our knowledge of vessel forms. The most common form for the Addis-like paste vessels, both combed and incised with any of the motifs, is a restricted bowl. Other observed vessel forms for the Addis-like paste include simple bowls (some with rim lugs), carinated bowls, and jars. The jars generally appear to be standard "Mississippian" jars, but some may be short-necked jars. There is not yet enough information to say whether any of these forms are more or less common through time or across the divisional boundaries.

The coarse shell-tempered Choctaw pottery is of the type known as Mississippi Plain; it was made throughout the Mississippi period. The main distinguishing characteristic of Choctaw pottery of this type is its general coarseness and the abundance of the shell in it. The shell particles range from 2 to 6 mm across and often make up 15–30 percent of the matrix of the pottery (Carleton 1992). Decoration is usually limited to pinched and nicked rims with or without diagonal incised lines depending from them. Some sherds have a brushed appearance, but this is probably due to dragging shell particles while smoothing the vessel exterior, and not to actual brushing. The vessel forms usually appear to be standard "Mississippian" jar forms, but some bowl forms might be present.

CERAMICS FROM ADJACENT AREAS

Lower/Central Pearl River Valley

Now let us compare the eighteenth-century Choctaw pottery with pottery from the adjacent areas identified earlier. The lower and central Pearl River valley has been somewhat neglected by archaeologists. One

Fig. 2. Examples of Anna Incised, A–B; Leland Incised, C–D; and Fatherland Incised, E–F (A–D after Phillips 1970, 102, 104; E–F after Neitzel 1983,
pl. 18).

of the few excavated sites there is the Pearl River Mounds (22Lw510),
which €yril B. Mann (1988) investigated for his master's thesis. This
site in Lawrence County, Mississippi, originally had at least fifteen
mounds and was occupied from about A.D. 1200 to about 1500–1600.
The site was probably the center for a substantial population, although
the people had disappeared from the area by the eighteenth century. The
decorated ceramics are predominantly Plaquemine grog-tempered
wares with Addis or Addis-like pastes; the undecorated ceramics are predominantly coarse shell-tempered Mississippi Plain. This unusual situation shows influences from both the Plaquemine cultures of the lower
Mississippi Valley and the Mississippian cultures to the north and east.
The most common late decoration present is what is known as Anna Incised (Figure 2; see Phillips 1970:102; S. Williams and Brain 1983:118–
20). Others motifs are related to those found on Leland Incised (Phillips
1970:104–7; S. Williams and Brain 1983:171–77; J. Brown 1985:295–
96) and Fatherland Incised (Phillips 1970:106; S. Williams and Brain
1983:175–77; J. Brown 1985:293–94). Also present are interesting
combinations of lower Mississippi Valley pastes with Tombigbee Valley
motifs such as Moundville Incised on a Plaquemine ware (C. B. Mann,
personal communication).

While most of the relevant decorative motifs from the Pearl River Mounds resemble the curvilinear/rectilinear motifs of the eighteenth-century Choctaw ceramics no more or less than other Natchezan motifs of the types mentioned above, the paste looks very similar to the Addis-like Choctaw ceramics. The Pearl River Mounds paste bears a marked resemblance to the paste found on Western Division sites, with the exception that there is no claystone added to the paste.

Upper Tombigbee River Valley/Black Prairie Region

The Upper Tombigbee/Black Prairie region has been the site of extensive archaeological investigations. Between the work done during the construction of the Tenn-Tom Waterway in the late 1970s and early 1980s and individual projects conducted by, among others, archaeologists from Mississippi State University, we have an extremely good picture of the prehistory of this area. While not as complete as the other periods, our picture of the late prehistoric and protohistoric periods for this area is fairly good. There was a relatively large late Mississippian and protohistoric population centered on the Lyon's Bluff site (22OK501) in Oktibeha County from about A.D. 1100 to 1550 (R. A. Marshall, personal communication). There was also a protohistoric/ historic population at the Rolling Hills site (22Ok593) in Starkville, Mississippi, which recent work by Richard A. Marshall (1992) indicates may be late seventeenth century.

The ceramics of the sixteenth- and seventeenth-century components of both sites are basically the same (Atkinson 1975, 1979; R. A. Marshall, personal communication). They are characterized by very sandy paste wares tempered with live shell and locally abundant fossil shell. The decoration is roughly incised, with usually curvilinear but occasionally rectilinear motifs mainly restricted to the shoulder and rims of vessels (Figure 3). The curvilinear motifs are usually arches, and the rectilinear motifs are nested boxed and diagonal lines, occasionally depending from punctations. The vessel forms include caswellas, restricted bowls, shallow bowls, and globular jars. This material, particularly that from Rolling Hills, has been associated with the Chakchiuma (Atkinson 1975, 1979; Marshall 1992). The ceramics generally bear little resemblance to those observed from the eighteenth-century Choctaw area. The extremely sandy paste is more like eighteenth-century Chickasaw ceramics than Choctaw (Atkinson 1979:61–64); however,

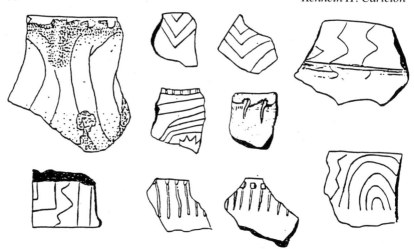

Fig. 3. Ceramics from the Rolling Hills site, 220k593 (after Atkinson 1979).

some of the rectilinear motifs are extremely similar to rectilinear punctate motifs used by the Choctaw.

Central Tombigbee/Black Warrior River Valley

The Central Tombigbee/Black Warrior Valley area had an enormous
late Mississippian (i.e., Moundville) and protohistoric population. The
occupations before the seventeenth century have been very well documented; unfortunately, only a few seventeenth- and eighteenth-century
sites have been located. During the protohistoric and historic periods
this area was occupied by people of the Alabama River phase (c. A.D.
1500–1700). The ceramics of this phase in the Tombigbee drainage
are characterized by pastes tempered with shell and mixed shell and
grog (Mann 1983:30). Decoration is predominantly incised with nested
arches, interlocking nested arches, and representational motifs (e.g.,
hands and long bones; see Figure 4; Mann 1983:36–40). The tempering agents are the same as some used by the Choctaw in the eighteenth
century but not as diverse. The nonrepresentational incised motifs are
vaguely similar to some used by the Choctaw, in that they are composed
of simple nested and interlocking nested figures, but these are motifs

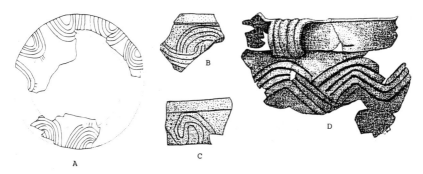

Fig. 4. Alabama River Incised. A–C, variety *Alabama River;* D, variety unspecified (after Mann 1983, figs. 11, 13, 15).

common to the protohistoric and historic from the Mississippi River valley to central Alabama.

Mobile-Tensaw Delta/Lower Tombigbee River Valley

Although extensive archaeological studies have been conducted in the Mobile-Tensaw Delta and along the lower Tombigbee, few seventeenth- and eighteenth-century sites have been located in the lower portion of this area. There was a notable sixteenth-century population in the area, as shown by the Bottle Creek site (1Ba2), and it is well known that the area was occupied at the time of initial European settlement by such groups as the Mobile, Tohomé, Chatot, and Naniaba, among others. Our best evidence for the seventeenth century, however, is north of Mobile Bay, from the lower Tombigbee and lower Alabama rivers in the area known as the Forks region. Several late sixteenth- and seventeenth-century sites have been found in this area, including the Pine Log site (1Ba462), the Doctor Lake site (1Ck219), the Douglas site (1Ck217), and the Ginhouse Island site (1Wn86). In addition, several late prehistoric and historic archaeological complexes have been described for this area, including the Bear Point Complex, the Ginhouse Island Complex, the Doctor Lake Complex, the Port Dauphin Complex, and the Guillary Complex (Fuller 1992). Of particular interest to this discussion are the Doctor Lake Complex and the Bear Point Complex.

The Doctor Lake Complex is estimated to date between A.D. 1650 and 1750, and while its complete distribution is currently unknown it is

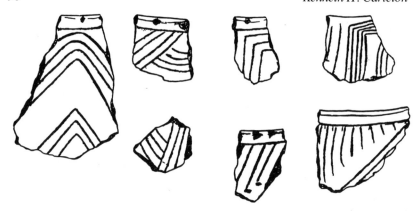

Fig. 5. Doctor Lake Incised (after Fuller et al. 1984, fig. 47).

definitely present in the Forks region, has been observed along Mobile
Bay, and probably extends up the Tombigbee River (Fuller 1992). The
ceramics associated with this complex are currently limited to two types,
Three Rivers Plain and Doctor Lake Incised, both of which are homogeneous, fine, sand-tempered wares, with occasional fine shell (Fuller
et al. 1984:225). Although the data are limited, vessel forms appear to
be primarily restricted bowls and possibly jars. The decoration (on Doctor Lake Incised) is fine line incising often with fingernail punctations
along the rim (Figure 5). Motifs are generally rectilinear in nature and
include nested boxes and diagonal lines with or without punctations.

While the paste of Doctor Lake ceramics is unlike that of Choctaw
ceramics, the motifs on Doctor Lake Incised are identical with or closely
related to some Choctaw motifs, particularly the rectangular punctate
and some of the geometric motifs (Fuller et al. 1984:226). Based on
decoration, almost all the Doctor Lake Incised sherds illustrated by
Richard Fuller, Diane Silvia, and Noel Stowe (1984:226, Figure 47)
could have been found on an eighteenth-century Choctaw site in central
Mississippi.

The Bear Point Complex dates from about A.D. 1550–1700 and is
widely distributed in southwestern Alabama (Fuller 1992). Two relevant
characteristic ceramic types associated with this complex are Pensacola
Incised and Mississippi Plain variety *Pine Log,* numerous whole vessels
of which were found at the Pine Log site (1BA462; see Stowe et al.
1982). A number of the motifs used on these Pensacola Incised vessels

are very similar to or have elements similar to some or both of the geo-metric and curvilinear/rectilinear motifs used by the Choctaw. This is particularly true of the motifs on the Pensacola Incised varieties *Pensacola, Bear Point,* and *Moore* vessels found at the Pine Log site (Stowe et al. 1982:21–34; see Figure 6). Mississippi Plain variety *Pine Log,* a coarse shell-tempered ware, uses a paste very similar to the coarse shell-tempered ceramics made by the Choctaw in the eighteenth cen-tury. The primary similarity is in the abundance and coarseness of the shell used, which is unusual. This is the only variety I have observed that approaches both the coarseness and the abundance of shell in the Choctaw ceramics.

A number of similarities have been noted between the Choctaw ceramics and ceramics found in areas adjacent to the Choctaw home-land. These similarities are primarily evident in two facets of the ceram-ics: paste and decorative motifs.

The Addis-like paste(s) used by the eighteenth-century Choctaw is most similar to that used by the Natchezan cultures in the lower Mis-sissippi Valley in the sixteenth through eighteenth centuries and by the people who lived at the Pearl River Mounds on the central Pearl River in the sixteenth century. Of these two areas, the ceramics from Pearl River Mounds most closely resembles that from the Choctaw homeland. The pastes from the eighteenth-century Choctaw most closely resemble that observed from Western Division sites in Neshoba County.

Examination of the motifs yields a more confused picture. The closest similarity to the curvilinear/rectilinear motif of the Choctaw is found in the Natchezan cultures of the lower Mississippi and central Pearl rivers; however, there are also some similarities to at least some of the motifs used on the Pensacola series ceramics from the lower Tombigbee and Mobile Bay region.

The geometric and rectilinear punctate motifs used by the eighteenth-century Choctaw are most similar to those from the Doctor Lake Com-plex in the lower Tombigbee and upper Mobile region. These motifs are nearly identical with some observed among the Choctaw, particularly those of the Eastern and Sixtowns divisions. There are also some simi-larities between the geometric and rectilinear punctate motifs and some of the motifs or their elements used on the Pensacola series ceramics in southwestern Alabama.

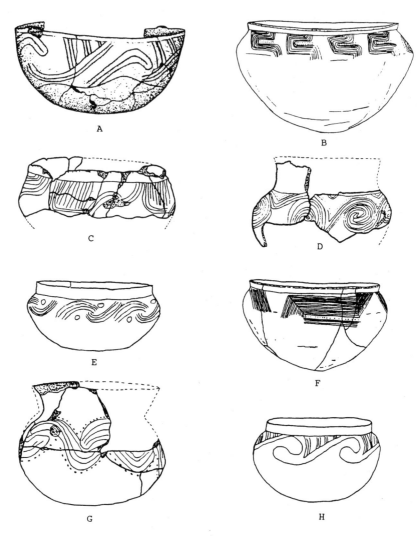

Fig. 6. Pensacola Incised. A from the Douglas site (1Ck217); B–H from the Pine Log site (1Ba462) (A after Fuller et al. 1984, fig. 16; B–H after Stowe et al. 1982, vessel nos. 1, 2, 10, 20, 29, 33, 37).

So, what does all this mean? The picture that emerges is of a mixing of elements, particularly paste manufacture (i.e., technology) and decorative motifs within the eighteenth-century Choctaw. This is completely consistent with Galloway's idea of a confederation of diverse people moving into the vacant area of central Mississippi to form what became the Choctaw. I believe that the similarities between the paste from the Pearl River Mounds and material from sites in the Western Division, and particularly the near absence of both the rectilinear punctate motif and the geometric motifs from the Western Division samples, indicate a western origin for the antecedents of the Western Division. The strong resemblance between the rectilinear punctate and the geometric motifs, most commonly found in the Eastern and Southern divisions, and the Doctor Lake Complex material indicates an eastern origin for the antecedents of these divisions.

The curvilinear/rectilinear motifs used by the eighteenth-century Choctaw resemble both the Natchezan motifs of the lower Mississippi and central Pearl rivers and the Pensacola series motifs of the lower Tombigbee and upper Mobile region. The curvilinear/rectilinear motifs used by the Choctaw are uniquely their own, however, and increasingly dominate motifs used through the eighteenth century across all divisions. By the end of the eighteenth century, and particularly in the nineteenth century, virtually all Addis-like ceramics made by the Choctaw employed the curvilinear/rectilinear motifs exclusively. Perhaps this indicates a fusion of shared motifs, and hence beliefs and identity, and a continued integration of diverse peoples into a single society well past initial confederation.

Leadership Nomenclature Among Spanish Florida Natives and Its Linguistic and Associational Implications

John H. Hann

Before about 1980 scholars gave little attention to leadership elements among the natives of Spanish Florida and changes they underwent between the first contacts in the sixteenth century and the dispersal or destruction of most of the tribal groups in the core area by 1705. Despite recent notable progress, the old Spanish sources have more to say on this topic than modern works, even about aspects as basic as native leadership nomenclature, which is the subject of this essay. I focus on the peoples of the core area with whom the Spaniards maintained contact between 1565 and 1704: the Timucua, Apalachee, and Chacato of north Florida and south Georgia; the Guale, Yamasee, and Tama of north Georgia; and the Escamacu and other peoples of the South Carolina coast (Figure 1). I will compare the nomenclature used in this core area with that revealed for the northern periphery by the Juan Pardo expeditions and that used for and by the Calusa and other natives of the southern periphery.

Caution is in order, of course, as our knowledge of native leadership nomenclature comes almost exclusively from Spanish and French sources rather than directly from the natives themselves. Native usage is often cloaked by the Spaniards' preference for the Arawak terms *cacique* and *cacica* for 'chief' and 'chieftainess' and for the Spanish term *mandador* 'order-giver' for the second in command in many areas. By the late seventeenth century even some literate Apalachee principal chiefs were calling themselves "cacique" to identify their position.

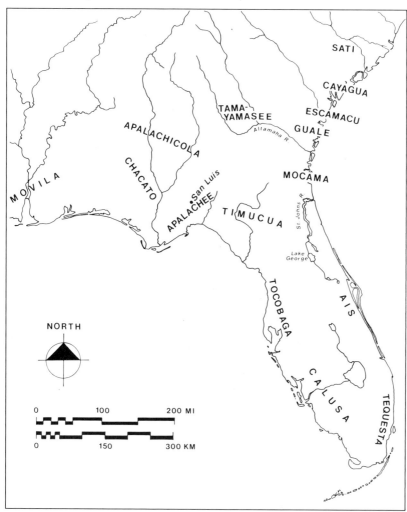

Fig. 1. Distribution of native peoples in Spanish Florida (prepared by Charles Poe).

TERMS USED FOR CHIEFS

For chieftains, Spaniards and Frenchmen and, in a few instances, natives themselves speaking directly used the terms *parucusi, paraousti, holata, utina, cacique principal* or *mayor, cacique, mico mayor, mico, king,* and *governor.* All but *cacique* and *governor* usually signified a 'head chief' who had other chiefs under his jurisdiction. In some cases the terms *holata, utina, cacique mayor,* and *mico mayor* signified a paramount chief. Of the terms native to Spanish Florida, *parucusi* and *holata* were the earliest to appear.

Parucusi as applied to living native rulers was the first term to appear and also the first to disappear. De Soto chroniclers used the title in forms such as *paracoxi* and *hurriparacoxi* for a chief belonging to the Safety Harbor Culture living twenty or thirty leagues inland from Tampa Bay. This chief received tribute from other chiefs who lived on or close to the bay (Elvas 1932, 2:46; Fernández de Oviedo y Valdés 1851, 1:549; Hernández de Biedma 1857:48). In the forms *paraousti* and *paracousi* René Laudonnière applied the title to various Timucua-speaking leaders living along the St. Johns River from its mouth to the vicinity of Lake George. He used the form *paraousti* first, while telling of his meeting with an unidentified chief at Matanzas Inlet, noting that it meant 'king and superior'. He first used *paracousi* in recording his initial encounter with Chief Saturiwa, observing that "the Paraousti took me by the hand . . . and showed me by signs the limits upriver of his dominion and told me that he was named Paracousi Satouriona. . . . The children bear the same title of Paraousti." Laudonnière used the two forms interchangeably both as a title for specific chiefs and as a general name for chiefs. Thus he alluded to "the Paraousti of the River of May," "Paracousi Molona," "Paracousi Outina," and "Ouae Outina, this great paracousi." But whether by accident or design, Laudonnière did not use either form for chiefs living north of the St. Johns River, who were Timucua speakers, or for the inland Timucua of Potano, Onatheaqua, or Houstaqua (Lussagnet 1958:86–90, 94, 104, 105, 110, 112, 113, 115, 116).

After de Soto's time Spaniards never applied the title to a specific ruler, but it appears as *ano parucusi holata yco* and *vtina parucusi holata,* respectively, in Fray Francisco Pareja's 1612 and 1627 catechisms, suggesting that it remained in use nonetheless. The French of the 1560s like the later English used the title king rather freely for native leaders, in contrast to Spaniards, who used that title consistently only for the Calusa head chief and even then only grudgingly. *Parucusi* also meant 'prince' or 'war prince', particularly in its form *urriparacoxi* (Granberry 1989:179; Lorant 1965:11). Except for the de Soto usage, *parucusi* appears to have been a term peculiar to Timucua speakers.

Holata, by contrast, was widely used. It was found in the mission provinces of Timucua and Apalachee and later among Creek and Choctaw. Apalachee and other members of the Muskogean family spelled it *holahta*. Juan de la Bandera applied this title in the form *orata* to more than one hundred leaders in the territory traversed by Juan Pardo and his men from coastal Escamacu to the deep hinterland of the Carolinas and Tennessee (Hudson 1990:62, 211–49). Only for the Guale and Tama-Yamasee is there lack of clear evidence of Spanish or native usage of *holata* as a title for chief; but such a usage among the Guale is suggested by the word's appearance in the names of towns such as Olatapotoque (Swanton 1922:83, 480).

Holata was first recorded in de Soto's time among the Timucua-speaking Potano joined to the name of a village near present-day Gainesville as Itaraholata (Fernández de Oviedo y Valdés 1851, 1:551). Laudonnière applied the title to Saturiwa's principal rival, Olata Ouae Outina, a head chief whose domain lay along the upper St. Johns River north of Lake George. But Laudonnière also called Ouae Outina "paracousi" (Lussagnet 1958:102, 112, 115). Fray Pareja used *holata* early in the seventeenth century as the equivalent of *cacique* (Milanich and Sturtevant 1972:67). No Spaniard appears to have used the term in mission times in speaking of a specific chief among the Timucua or Apalachee; however, some literate chiefs among both peoples appended the title to their names in signing. Thus a chief from Alta Timucua signed his name Lázaro Chamile Holatama (Rebolledo 1657:106). The *-ma* is a Timucua suffix meaning 'the', or the possessive 'his', 'her', and 'my', which appears also in the titles *utinama* and *inihama* (Granberry 1989:117).

We do not know what indigenous title ordinary Apalachee chiefs bore before or during mission times. Late in the mission era "cacique" was used almost exclusively by Spaniard and Indian alike, with head chiefs at mission centers being known as "principal caciques." Chiefs who signed a 1688 letter in the Apalachee language appended "cacique" to their names, except for Ivitachuco's head chief, who was the paramount.

He signed his name "Do^n Be[ntu]^{ra} ybitachuco *holahta*." Evidence elsewhere in the letter suggests that in Apalachee *holahta* connoted 'great chief'. The chiefs used the term to designate the king of Spain as their "great chief" thus, "*pin holahta chuba pin Rey*" (literally, 'our chief great, our King'). They also gave the Spanish governor the title *holahta* (Chiefs of Apalachee 1688; Leturiondo 1677; Florencia 1694).

Holahta did not have that exalted sense among all members of the Muskogean family. Jerald T. Milanich and William C. Sturtevant (1972: 49, n. 13) noted that the Creek *holahta* was "the title of an official less important than a *mi'kko* or town chief." Charles Hudson (1990:61–62) observed that Juan de la Bandera, chronicler of the Pardo expeditions, defined an *orata* as a minor lord and a *mico* as a great lord. Hudson concluded that three levels of chiefly authority were discernible among people with whom Pardo had dealings. "From highest to lowest," he noted, "the three levels were *orata, mico,* and grand chief." Bandera recorded no indigenous term for the latter position. Hudson noted further that oratas headed even tiny ramshackle communities. To accentuate further the lowly status of some of Bandera's oratas, Hudson might also have noted that Bandera gave the title orata even to officials below the level of chief, the *inijas*. But even taking that application into consideration, Bandera's statements may not justify as sweeping a conclusion about the relative status of oratas and micos as the one Hudson proposed.

Elsewhere, when Bandera first mentioned the title *orata*, he explained that it signified 'great lord'. He reinforced that definition a little farther on. When he listed thirteen oratas who met Pardo at Canos (Cofitachequi), he described them as "very principal chiefs" while noting that there were "many others who are subjects and under the domination of some of the above-mentioned" thirteen oratas. Thus he indicated that oratas could be head chiefs. Canos orata undoubtedly was one.

Conversely, in the example Hudson cited in positing the inferiority of oratas, Bandera did not necessarily put oratas in general in the inferior position suggested by Hudson, but possibly only one whom Bandera introduced as "*orata chiquini*" in explaining the meaning of mico on his first use of that title (Hudson 1990:211, 212–13, 215, 260). In view of Bandera's earlier statement that an orata was a great lord, probably all one can conclude from the statement is that an orata qualified as "chiquini" (or named Chiquini) was "less a lord" vis-à-vis the mico of Guatari, but not that all oratas were inferior to micos, nor that everywhere oratas appeared there was a mico to rule over them. Micos appeared only after Pardo had passed beyond what Hudson believed to be Muskogean territory. For most of the territory Pardo traversed, the terms *mico* and *orata* were not juxtaposed. Furthermore, it is not clear that the numerous oratas who met with Pardo at the seat of leaders like Joara mico were subject to the micos. Bandera identified only three micos in comparison with the more than one hundred oratas he mentioned, and all three micos were bunched in the northern part of that territory.

Turning now to the term *utina,* Milanich (1978:71) identified this as "a Timucuan word meaning chief or king," noting that its "usage might have been widespread through the area in which Timucuan was spoken." Nevertheless, it appears infrequently in the records, and only among Timucua speakers. It first appears in the de Soto chronicles as Utinama and Utinamocharra, variant names for the third Potano village through which de Soto passed, and as Uriutina for a village in the province of Utina (Elvas 1932:33; Fernández de Oviedo y Valdés 1951:551–52). A mission village, Santa Isabel de Utinahica, also bore the name. The chiefly title *utina* is probably reflected also in the name Outina or Hotina given to a Freshwater Timucua head chief in French and Spanish sources from the 1560s (Lussagnet 1958; Solís de Merás 1923:202, 203, 206). Fray Pareja appears to be the only other primary chronicler who mentioned *utina* as a chiefly title, in the form *utina parucusi holata* (Pareja 1627). Albert S. Gatschet (1878:492) considered *utinama* one of the titles applied to upper-echelon chiefs. His belief is borne out by non-Christian Timucuas' use of Utinama to refer to the Christians' God (Oré 1936:106–7).

Mico is the last of the indigenous terms used for chiefs. For the Guale, Tama, and Yamasee of north Georgia, Spaniards regularly used the terms *mico* and *mico mayor* to designate chief and head chief, whereas they avoided the use of the terms *holata, parucusi,* or any other indigenous title for the leaders of other peoples in the mission territories. *Mico* and *mico mayor* seem generally to have been reserved for leaders of the more important Guale settlements, while chiefs of less important settlements were referred to exclusively as caciques (Argüelles 1677; Ibarra 1604:177–91; Lanning 1935:82–111; Pueyo 1695). At the time of the Spaniards' first definite contact with the Guale, they identified Tolomato's chief as "the supreme lord [who] is called mico, which is like king or prince of that land in that tongue" (Zubillaga 1946:587).

In the mission provinces, *mico* was a language-specific title. Guale, Tama, Yamasee, and the Lower Creek peoples whom Spaniards identified as Apalachicola shared the title and spoke either the same language or mutually intelligible variants. In 1568 a Jesuit described the Guales' language as the most universal one that he had learned of in Florida, as it was understood for two hundred leagues into the hinterland (Zubillaga 1946:325). The validity of his judgment was confirmed a century later in the person of Diego Camuñas, an interpreter whom Spaniards employed for dealings with Guale and Yamasee living on the coast and with Apalachicola living along the Chattahoochee. In the 1680s a Yamasee spying for the Spaniards remarked that in the vicinity of the village of Apalachicola he was able to pass as a local when he dressed as the locals did because people there found nothing unusual in his language and because he understood their language very well (Argüelles 1677; Matheos 1686, 1688; Pueyo 1695). Micos are not mentioned for any of the other missionized provinces. Nothing can be said with certainty about the linguistic affiliation of the three micos mentioned by Bandera for Joara, Guatari, and Olameco in the northern reaches of the territory Pardo traversed (Hudson 1990:262, 265, 267). Hudson (1990:83) speculated that they might be speakers of Catawba, Iroquoian, or Yuchi.

The terms *cacique* and *king* were mentioned for chiefs of the south Florida tribes, but no indigenous term appears in the records. "Great captain" is the one distinctive title Spaniards used when speaking of south Florida native leaders. The great captain was the second in command and controlled the military. He was usually a brother or close relative of the head chief. Great captains appeared as well among the Tocobaga to the north of the Calusa and among the Ais of the east coast. Spaniards never used the term *great captain* for leadership elements of the mission provinces and never employed terms found farther north, such as *holata, mico,* or *inija,* for south Florida leaders. In general, south Florida seems to have been a world apart from the rest of Spanish Florida in many ways. This suggests that the sharing of leadership nomenclature was linked to the sharing of other culture features and that the leadership nomenclature of the peoples from north Florida northward into the Appalachian Mountains reflects a more advanced stage of development than that of south Florida's cultures.

TERMS FOR THE SECOND IN COMMAND

Inija was the most widely used native name for the second in command. Its distribution may even have surpassed that of *holata,* as the *inija* was recorded for the Guale and Chacato as well as for the Apalachee, Timucua, and, later, Creek. Its use among still other people may be concealed under the Spanish term *mandador.* The inija was first mentioned in the 1560s in Pardo's far northern hinterland. At Tocae, Pardo met two ynahaes oratas whom Bandera described thus in a parenthetical note, *"ynihaEs* are like what we might call justices or *Jurados* who command the people" (Hudson 1990:230, 276). Hudson noted that Bandera also described an *yniha* at Olameco as "like a 'sheriff' who commands the town" (*"como alquazil q. manda el pueblo"*) (Hudson 1990:65, 115, n. 37).

Bandera's explanations capture more or less the role inijas played in the mission provinces, where they were village administrators responsible for seeing that essential tasks were attended to. They spoke for the village in dealings with outsiders in the absence of the chief. In Apalachee they also were repositories of tribal lore and myths and information on inheritance rights to chiefships. The inija's position was hereditary, like that of the chief (Hann 1988:106). Although large mission centers like San Luis in Apalachee had more than one inija and deputies to the inija known as *chacales,* there is no evidence for Apalachee of an equivalent to the Enehau Ulgee, or collective inija-ship that Benjamin Hawkins (1982:15) portrayed as occupying the mico's cabin on the left in the Creek square ground and being in charge of the town's public works (like the Spanish Florida inija) and preparation of the black drink. But Pareja's (1612) description of the lineages that provided counsellors for Timucuan head chiefs possibly indicates a collective inija-ship for that people in the persons of the *ynihama, anacotimas, asetama, yvitano, toponole, ybichara,* and *amalachini.* When the chief did not wish to take the counsel offered by the ynihama, he turned to the anacotima as an alternate. The Timucuan ynihama, described by Pareja as "a counsellor who brings the Cacique near at hand [*a la mano*]," emerged from the lineage of the head chief.

Although the records mention inijas for all the mission provinces, the title is recorded less frequently for the Guale and Timucua than for the Apalachee. That may be only an accident of the records, of course.

Guale and Timucua references more frequently mention mandadores. In many instances it is likely that the Spaniards' mandador was the inija, as *mandador*'s meaning, 'order-giver', expresses the essence of the inija's duties. A soldier in Apalachee made that identification clear, testifying that the deputy governor there "broke the head of Bi Bentura, *enija* of the village of San Luis, who is *mandador,* second person to the cacique" (Matheos 1688). But *mandador* and *inija* were not coterminous. In the first explicit mention of an inija for Guale that I have encountered, Florida's governor addressed an order to the "caciques, Ynijas, and mandadores" of the province (Ruiz de Salazar Vallecilla 1650). For the coastal peoples, however, when an inija was not mentioned and an official was identified as a mandador, it is likely that he was an inija. In Guale, *mandador* may also have referred at times to the *alaiguita,* whose duties and status may well have paralleled the inija's in a manner similar to the Timucuas' anacotima. In 1695 a Guale leader named Agustín was alluded to as mandador on one occasion and as alaiguita on another. When Spaniards addressed their orders to the "caciques, Ynijas, and mandadores," it is probable that the mandadores were alaiguitas. Spaniards used the term *mandador* most frequently when speaking of coastal peoples from Georgia northward.

Mandador was a particularly common term in the South Carolina region at the beginning of the seventeenth century, and it seems to have been applied to officials other than inijas. For the Escamacu, Cayagua, and Sati, Spaniards used "cacique" for chiefs and "mandador" and "mandador mayor" for officials below the level of chief, who, at times, were heads of outlying settlements (Fernández de Ecija 1605, 1609). Bandera used "mandador" similarly for the hinterland in the 1560s (Hudson 1990:66). In 1609 Francisco Fernández de Ecija said of his entrance onto the Jordan River [the Santee], "And going inland from the two headlands there is a large river, which we ascended until we reached some cabins and fields sown with corn, where an Indian lived, who was the *mandador,* which is what we call those [i.e., the leaders] of the Jordan" (Fernández de Ecija 1609:26). He noted subsequently that the mandador's chief, named Sati, lived in a village some distance upriver.

OTHER LEADERSHIP TERMS

Gobernador (governor) was another Spanish term applied frequently to native leaders. The native "governor" was a person in charge of the village in the place of a chief when that chief was incapable of exercising the duties of the office because of old age, illness, mental incapacity, or other causes. In a 1695 visitation it was recorded that Mico Bernabé of Tupiqui had been removed earlier as ruling mico at the request of other village leaders and replaced by Tupiqui's alaiguita, who was then given the title "governor" by the Spanish governor who authorized this change (Pueyo 1695). More commonly, nephew or niece heirs to a chieftainship were installed as governors when their ruling aunt or uncle was incapacitated (Florencia 1695). It is not clear whether the practice had a formalized native equivalent or was introduced by Spaniards. Among the Calusa, who did not recognize Spanish sovereignty, old chiefs seem simply to have stepped aside at a certain point in favor of a son (Hann 1991:165–67, 222–23, 267–68).

Guale is the only province known to have had a special title, *tunaque*, for the heir to a chiefship. Frequent mention of Guale heirs in documents addressed to the leaders, in contrast with the practice for most other provinces, suggests that Guale heirs had more of a special status and possibly more of a leadership role than such heirs did elsewhere. A special seat was reserved for the tunaque in the council house. Similar mention of such heirs occurred to some degree in Mocama, a coastal Timucua province immediately south of Guale, although no such special title is known for Mocama heirs (Argüelles 1677:525; Ibarra 1604:171, 176, 178–79, 183–84, 188). As the Mocama shared other aspects of the culture of their northern neighbors, this was probably but one more instance of such influence.

The Apalachee, Chacato, and Creek had a special term, *usinulo* 'beloved son', for one of the ruling chief's sons. The title is not recorded for the Timucua or Guale. Special roles in ceremonies associated with the Apalachees' ball game were reserved to the usinulo (the Creek spelled it *usinjulo;* see Fernández de Florencia 1675; Hann 1988:104, 123, 338, 340).

Little or nothing is known about the remaining officials referred to as *principales* (leading men), *ibisache,* and *chacales.* The term *ibisache,* which denotes a Guale official, is mentioned only once. *Principales* was a catch-all term used by the Apalachee, Guale, and Timucua for counsellors below the rank of inija and noted warriors (Argüelles 1677; Leturiondo 1677). In Apalachee, chacales were most commonly deputies of the inija who performed functions such as overseeing work in the community fields. But the term was used at times to identify the inija himself, possibly to refer to one aspect of his duties. Vi Ventura, principal inija at San Luis de Apalachee from at least 1677, was referred to in 1695 by a fellow Indian, Mateo Chuba, who had once been governor at San Luis, as "the *Jinija* of San Luis and head *chacal.*" Spaniards employed the term *chacal* as well to refer to *fiscales*, even the fiscal for the Council of the Indies. The Timucua and the Chacato also had chacales, but their role among those people is not known as clearly. Pareja mentioned them in a question to be addressed to "caciques, mandadores and chacales" in the confessional, "Have you ordered that someone be punished by breaking his arm, not because of the work, but rather because you were irritated [*enojado*]," referring to the chacal with the form *chacalicarema* (Fernández de Florencia 1675; Florencia 1695; Hann 1988:106; Milanich and Sturtevant 1972:69).

Tascaia, noroco, and *nicoguadca* were warrior titles of ascending rank. A tascaia was an entry-level warrior recognized as having taken a scalp. A noroco had three scalps to his credit. Both titles are recorded for the Apalachee and Timucua. *Noroco* seems to have been used also in the sense of "citizen." *Nicoguadca* appears only in the Apalachee ball game manuscript. The word *tascaia* is mentioned in reference to the Chacato as well (Fernández de Florencia 1675; Hann 1988:71, 182, 343, 405; 1992:467). It appeared in the form *tasigaya* far to the north among the Indians with whom Moyano allied himself at Joara (Hudson 1990:27).

The wide circulation of leadership titles like holata and inija across tribal and linguistic frontiers suggests considerable sharing or borrowing of cultural elements by peoples living over a wide area extending from north Florida proper to at least as far north as North Carolina and Tennessee. Only the fishermen–hunter-gatherers of south Florida seem not to have participated at all in the nomenclature that characterized the mission provinces and to some degree territories far to the north of them. The Guale, Yamasee, and Tama stand apart to a degree from the other missionized peoples because of their use of *mico* and *mico mayor*. But they are bound to the rest through the term *inija*. The Guale may also share the term *holata*. All three share the mico-ship with the Creek and groups encountered by Pardo far to the north. The greater complexity of the Guale and Timucua's roster of named officials vis-à-vis the Apalachee is probably no more than an accident of documentation. Bandera's extensive use of the title orata raises questions whether it is entirely the equivalent of the holata of the Timucua and Apalachee. His application of orata to inijas is particularly questionable.

The Apalachee and Chacato stand apart from the other missionized peoples because of a total absence of women in chiefly positions. For the Chacato, of course, the time span for which we have records is minimal. The relatively little that is known about south Florida's peoples indicates an absence of female leadership there as well. In terms of shared political nomenclature the Apalachee and Chacato appear to have had close ties culturally, possibly reflecting conditions during the time of the Fort Walton culture when they may have been one people or more closely related. The absence of the mico-ship among them distinguishes them from their closest neighbors to the north, the Lower Creek eastward to the coastal Guale.

Identification of the mico-ship with peoples of north Georgia within the mission provinces and the Spaniards' tendency to identify micos by their proper title make the mico-ship a good marker for detecting migrations within the mission provinces. Heretofore, the appearance of Georgia-type ceramics at Timucua mission sites has sometimes led authorities to conclude that it signified a substantial movement of Guale or Yamasee into such sites. The absence of the mention of micos for such areas suggests that there was no substantial movement of Guale or Yamasee into Florida proper prior to 1702, except for a few documented cases, and that the earlier conclusions based on ceramics may need to be reconsidered. The documented exceptions are Tolomato's 1620s relocation to the vicinity of St. Augustine, the 1670s movement of Tama-Yamasee into Apalachee, and the resettlement of Yamasee and Guale on Amelia Island. The mico-ship's absence from Apalachee and western Timucua also suggests that the introduction of Lamar-type ceramics, known formerly as Leon-Jefferson, did not result from any substantial immigration from the Lamar heartland where the mico-ship prevailed. Tracing shared and unshared leadership nomenclature can provide valuable insights into relations between peoples and offers another tool by which archaeologists can test conclusions based principally or exclusively on archaeological sources.

Myth and Social History in
the Early Southeast

Greg Keyes

The ethnographic present—the assumption that southeastern Indians can be understood by creating a synchronic synthesis of all the data that exist about them from whatever dateline—has proved very persistent. But it is a paradigm that, by its very nature, cannot account for change. And the southeastern Indians have changed dramatically in the past five hundred years—socially, politically, linguistically, and in material culture. Though this change is now generally recognized and understood, our cognizance is rarely extended to include southeastern belief systems. Mythology is still captive to the ethnographic present, perceived as a timeless thing that can be lost through acculturation but which is, as long as it exists, absolutely conservative. This assumption is so deep-rooted that many scholars use nineteenth- and twentieth-century mythology and ceremony to interpret thirteenth-century iconography without the slightest hesitation (e.g., Howard 1968).

What is lacking for a critique of such endeavors is an understanding of which elements of southeastern Indian mythology are actually durable and which are subject to change. Thus the question posed here is this: Bearing in mind that a fundamental social transformation occurred in the late sixteenth-century Southeast, can we find any parallel transformations in the mythologies of the southeastern Indians? Did the people of the great chiefdoms of Apalachee, Coosa, and Cofitachequi tell the same stories and hold the same beliefs as their descendants who lived on reservations at the turn of this century? If not, then what changed about their mythology, and what remained constant? These questions are not tangential; they lie at the heart of the relationship between social structure and mythology, history and belief.

The Apalachee Ball Game myth presents us with an opportunity to explore these questions. Like most of their neighbors in the Southeast, the early Apalachee were politically organized as a chiefdom. Definitions of chiefdoms vary, but the consensus is that they are ranked societies with several levels of hierarchy and hereditary leadership. The contact-period Apalachee meet these criteria (Scarry 1990). In the 1670s, when the myth examined in this essay was recorded, the Apalachee were subject to Spanish rule through the mission system, but there is clear evidence that certain chiefdom-like characteristics remained, including hereditary succession to office and differential access to political and economic power (Scarry 1990:184–85). The myth collected by Friar Juan Paina is thus especially significant in that it was associated with at least a nominal chiefdom. As such, it belongs to a small corpus of similar myths, including those from the eighteenth-century Natchez and seventeenth-century Hasinais (see Swanton 1911, 1942).

In addition to having been collected at an early date, the Apalachee Ball Game myth is also quite rich in detail. Following is a brief summary of the myth.

Two chiefs, Ochuna Niko Watka[1] and Itonanslak, were neighbors. Both were identified by the Apalachee as "demons" (or so it seemed to Paina). The name Itonanslak translates as 'Person of Banked Fires' or perhaps 'Old Person with (or in) the Fire'.[2] Ochuna Niko Watka means 'The Lightning' (Hann 1988:331).

Itonanslak had a granddaughter known as Niko Tayholo (Wife of the Sun, or Woman Beloved of the Sun).[3] Sent by the old men of the town to gather water each day, she became mysteriously pregnant while doing so. She concealed her pregnancy, gave birth to the child in the woods, and abandoned it. The child, found by a panther, bear, and blue jay, was taken to Itonanslak, who swore the animals to secrecy and raised the boy as his own. The boy went through several name changes: first called Chita, he was later renamed Oklafi (Water Person or Baron of the Water) and still later, as a young man, Eslafiayupi. Eslafiayupi excelled in sports and physical exercises.

The other chief, Niko Watka, noticed this boy and became concerned. A prophecy foretold his death at the hands of a child of Niko Tayholo, and despite all precautions taken to protect Eslafiayupi's identity, he began to suspect that the boy was indeed the one foretold. Thus he tried to have the boy killed by requiring him to accomplish three dangerous tasks. Itonanslak had foreseen this possibility, and he had instructed the boy in ways to survive the tasks. When the three tests failed to kill Eslafiayupi, Niko Watka conceived of the ball game as an alternative way to do away with the boy. He sent a messenger dressed as a horned raccoon to tell Itonanslak the rules. Itonanslak in turn invented the ritual precautions to go with the game.

On the day the ball game was to be played, the two teams came into the plaza, painted as animals: the men on Itonanslak's team were painted as bears, wolves, and other strong, "dark creatures." Those playing for Niko Watka were dressed as deer and other such animals. Eslafiayupi was leaning against a tree, dressed in a cloak of feathers, looking ill. When called to join the game he did so, scoring point after point. On the seventh score he let out a shout like thunder, and on doing so was recognized as Niko Watka, the Flash of Lightning,[4] son of Niko Tayholo and the Sun.

Now more rivalrous than ever, the elder Niko Watka challenged his young namesake to a game of *kisiyo,* the Apalachee version of chunky. The two men gambled on the outcome of the game, and the younger won everything, including the elder's life. At this point the Spanish text becomes confused: one of the two Niko Watkas, logically the elder, tried to escape by claiming he needed to get a drink of water and to relieve himself. His opponent gratified these needs by striking the earth with his kisiyo pole, calling up a spring and a grove of trees, each to serve one of the pretended needs. The Niko Watka who made these requests (again, probably the elder) then fabricated a further excuse to go into his house, escaped through a back way, and fled to Apalachicola. The other (probably younger) Niko Watka pursued him with many warriors, overcame mists and magical traps, slew his namesake, and returned.

Many years later, Niko Watka felt that his time had come to die. He ordered his people to boil him in a pot, so that he would ascend in a cloud to become thunder and lightning. He told his people that any one of them could become niko watka if they could slay seven warriors and three *hitas tascaiyas* (warriors of rank; see Hann 1988:331–53).

It is immediately obvious that this is more than merely an entertaining story. The protagonists are chiefs and the progeny of chiefs, and are furthermore identified by Paina as "demons." We can assume, given the obvious bias of the good friar, that we could substitute "gods" or "spirits" for "demons." Whatever the case, they clearly represent supernatural forces: Itonanslak is the personification of Fire, a pervasive spiritual force in most, if not all, southeastern belief systems (Swanton 1928:213; Hudson 1976:317–18). Niko Watka is Lightning, and his name contains the word *niko*, the Apalachee word for 'sun'. Furthermore, the mother of the protagonist is clearly identified as the wife of the Sun, and her child, Eslafiayupi-cum-Niko Watka, is the child of the Sun. Eslafiayupi is thus great-grandson of the Old-Man-in-the-Fire and son of the solar deity.

The heros and antagonists of this story established social institutions. The elder Niko Watka invented the ball game itself, and Itonanslak created the ceremonial accouterments of the game. Perhaps most interestingly, the younger Niko Watka instituted the qualifications for the position of niko watka once he departed. The name of this hero is thus the name of the social position. Exactly what privileges and powers the temporal niko watka enjoyed are not known, but Paina was persuaded that there was a real man who held the title.

As my children have told me, those from San Luis, that not long ago there died an Indian named Talapagna Luis, who had a staff or club the size of a *benoble*. And, on the tip of the said pole some scalps, and some painted. And I asked who [or possibly what] that was. And they told me that he [or it] was Itatascaia and now they have confessed to me that he was Nicoguadca.

While I was priest of this *doctrina*, the year of seventy-one, I left [to become] the guardian of the convent of St. Augustine. And, during this time, while the Reverend Fray Francisco Maillo was its priest, this Indian died, and they still tell me he said that he would have to come back and burn the ball post. As though by the just judgements of God Our Lord, a lightning bolt fell that year and burned that [the ball post] of San Luis. (Hann 1988:343)

This is a clear indication that there was a position within the Apalachee hierarchy called niko watka, and also that this office was supposed to have the powers of the mythical Niko Watka attached to it. The myth, then, can be seen as a sort of supernatural charter for the living niko watka. The other central characters may or may not also be archetypes for political positions; Itonanslak, whose name means 'Old Man in the Fire', seems to have affinities with the concept of Fire as ruler, exemplified most clearly in eighteenth-century Natchez belief. The Great Sun, ruler of the Natchez, was called Owa'shi'l, literally, 'Superlative Flame' (Swanton 1911:168). Eighteenth-century Chickasaw priests were known as *loachi*, meaning "men resembling the Holy Fire" (Adair and Williams 1974:84).[5]

As for Ochuna Niko Watka, the elder of the two Niko Watkas, he may represent an aging version of the younger, and the myth may be a blueprint for the succession to office of one niko watka by another. This speculation aside, we can note three things about this myth:

1. The major characters are deified and elite in the context of the myth's society.
2. The myth chartered at least one real social position in the Apalachee power structure.
3. Ceremonies performed by the Apalachee had their origins accounted for by these mythic characters.

Other myths from this early era perform similar functions. For instance, a Natchez myth establishes the lineage of Suns, relating them to the solar deity. The same story rationalizes Natchez temples, Sacred Fire, and the descent system (Swanton 1911:169–72).

Having identified a few salient aspects of early southeastern myth, can we now find any similarities with myths collected in the nineteenth and twentieth centuries? I examined some eight hundred southeastern myth texts, all collected from southeastern Indians and found through an exhaustive search of published and unpublished materials. In my search for parallels I posed questions based on the three statements made above about the Apalachee Ball Game myth: Are the actors in the myths gods and members of a social elite? Are social positions chartered? Are ceremonies created?

To all but the last of these, the answer was uniformly no. For example, if we examine a representative nineteenth-century myth, the Tunica Thunder myth, collected by Albert Gatschet in 1880 (Swanton 1911:319–22) and again by Mary Haas in 1943 (Haas 1950:24–61), we find in it many of the same themes and motifs contained in the Apalachee Ball Game myth. A boy is raised by his uncle, who becomes angry because he thinks the boy disobeyed him. The uncle sends the boy out to perform two tasks designed to kill him. Interestingly enough, they are the same as two of the tasks that Eslafiayupi is sent to perform in the Apalachee story—to gather cane from a snake-infested canebrake and to invade the nest of a giant bird and steal something. In the Tunica story the boy is aided by Rabbit, the trickster, and by the bird itself. (Contrast this with the Apalachee story, in which the boy's great-grandfather advises him.) The boy is then stranded across the ocean, a motif lacking from the Apalachee Ball Game myth. When he returns from his exile, the boy defeats his antagonist (the uncle) and ascends into the sky as Thunder.

It is obvious that these stories have much in common, including the identification of the protagonist as a thunder deity. But in the Tunica story the hero exists in a social vacuum. He is not part of a town, and his antagonist is not a rival chief. His parents and origins are never mentioned, and he solves his problems with the help of various woodland beings rather than with that of his grandfather. When he is transformed into Thunder, he leaves no provisions for an earthly representative, nor does he create even one ceremony. The motifs of these stories are quite similar, but they imply very different social contexts and different uses within these contexts.

Almost every motif or story incident in the Apalachee Ball Game myth can be found in later stories. For example, in a Yuchi myth, a boy is revealed as the bastard son of Thunder, and he must play chunky and then a ball game against a monster called Red Copper (Wagner 1931:70–76). In a twentieth-century Natchez myth, a woman mysteriously conceives several children. One of her children is Thunder, who destroys her enemies in a ball game (Swanton 1929a:215–18). There are many other examples as well. On the basis of this comparison we can conclude that the motifs themselves are durable—that they probably existed before they were incorporated into the Apalachee myth and certainly persisted long afterward. But the *context* and social purpose of the myth—the use these motifs were assembled for—had vanished by the nineteenth century.

One of the three social "markers" identified in the Apalachee Ball Game myth *does*, however, occur in later stories: there are numerous examples of ceremonies being explained by myth. The Yuchi culture hero learned the rite of the emetic and other similar rituals in the rainbow squareground of the upper world (Speck 1909:106–7). The Tunica sun dance was performed because the solar deity, shamed by a spurned lover, danced her way into the sky, hung about with silver and singing the song that Mary Haas recorded in 1943 (Haas 1950:20–24). Cherokee botanical cures for certain diseases were predicated on the mythical relationships between people, animals, and plants in the ancient time (J. Mooney 1982:319–24).

A pattern emerges when these continuities and changes are viewed against the backdrop of social history. The Apalachee Ball Game myth is peopled with gods and elite-class characters. It created ceremony and social positions. This follows logically from the fact that the Apalachee had a power structure to maintain, and a legitimizing ideology is one tool for such maintenance. If mythology links the creation of ceremony to the elite, the position of the elite is further justified. Conversely, the Tunica of the twentieth century had no such hierarchy to maintain. They were a poor, marginal, rural people who lived in the swampy land near Marksville, Louisiana, and investing chiefs that had been dead for at least two centuries with mythological legitimacy was clearly not one of their priorities. Tunica myths other than the Thunder myth do nonetheless address some social needs. "Why the Tunica and Biloxi Became Friends" (Haas 1950:148–49) is a brief story that lays the post-facto mythical groundwork for the necessary cooperation of two small Indian tribes circumscribed by a vast sea of Anglo-Americans and Creoles. But there are no heaven-sent chiefs, no proscribed rules of divine right such as those found in the Apalachee and early Natchez myths.

The conclusion that myth is intimately attached to social structure seems obvious, but it is often overlooked by those who wish to reconstruct prehistoric belief systems from the fragments of the historic period. A case in point is the Mississippian chunky player motif. James Brown (1985:111–12) has tentatively interpreted this motif on the basis of a Cherokee myth in which two supernatural boys use a stone wheel to track their father. From this, Brown concludes that the chunky game may have served as a means of divination, the fallen stone and staves being "read" like knucklebones.

Perhaps. But the Cherokee in 1880 were almost half a millennium removed from the society that produced those gorgets and at least two hundred years removed from a chiefdom or chiefdom-like society. By 1880 chunky was only very vaguely remembered (J. Mooney 1982:434), and certainly whatever function it played in Mississippian society had long since been forgotten.[6] It seems more likely that the chunky player motif present in the Apalachee Ball Game myth—earlier, from a people still hierarchically organized and less than a century distant from a fully

Fig. 1. The Mississippian chunky player motif. Eddyville Gorget, Eddyville, Ky. (drawing by Steve Wooldridge).

functional chiefdom—provides a more valid explanation for the Mississippian engravings. Consider the running figure of the Eddyville gorget (Figure 1), grasping a staff with his human hand and a chunky stone with a great, taloned claw. Does it not seem much more like a representation of Niko Watka, Thunder god and warrior extraordinaire, engaging in a high-stakes elite competition than of two boys trying to find their father? Or a prognosticating priest mentioned in no story whatsoever?

   Attempts to explain the complex iconography of the Mississippian period using late nineteenth-century mythology should be viewed through a fine filter of skepticism. The persistence and recurrence of motifs means little if the context in which they were interpreted is not considered as well, and the Mississippian context largely faded away in the seventeenth century. Certainly the Southeastern Ceremonial Complex was associated with the social elite, and as this essay has endeavored to show, legitimizing ideologies of the elite vanish when the elite vanish. The *stories* may persist, but stripped of the special context and details that made them what they were. The motifs, informed by a new society with new needs, are reshuffled and restructured.

In the final analysis, we can never be certain of what prehistoric southeastern iconography "means." But we can try to understand how mythology and society are related and how change has affected them both. This southeastern example makes it clear that some aspects of mythology are very durable: motifs appear to resist the ravages of time like granite building blocks. But the castles and towers these blocks are used to build may tumble and be rearranged into humbler—or perhaps merely different—structures. A study of southeastern myth in the context of social history can show us something that the ethnographic present cannot: the persistent patterning and use of these mythological building blocks, how they are arranged and rearranged, and why.

NOTES

1. The precise orthography of these names varies somewhat in the original Spanish text, and I therefore chose to use Geoffrey Kimball's (1988) rendering of the Apalachee whenever possible.

2. Geoffrey Kimball identifies Nan Slak as 'old person' in his Apalachee vocabulary (1988). *Ito-* looks like a prefix found in Choctaw (*ito-*), Koasati (*itta-*), and Hichiti (*ita-*) that acts as a locative that means 'fire'; thus, Ito-nan-slak 'Old Person in or with the Fire' (these are my own comparisons and interpretations).

3. John Hann translates this as 'woman of the sun' (1988:331), but this is a translation of the original Spanish. The Apalachee here seems to mean 'wife of the sun' (Kimball 1988:395).

4. Kimball gives this as 'ray of the sun', perhaps a euphemism for lightning (Kimball 1988:395).

5. Cyrus Byington's Choctaw dictionary gives the noun form of *luachi* as 'a burner'. The verb signifies making or causing fire (Byington 1915:246).

6. There is also no historical precedent for the chunky game as a divina-

tory endeavor, and there are some very early references to it (e.g., Larson 1978:128–29). It was primarily a game of skill and usually involved gambling. Further, in another Cherokee version of the Wild Boy myth, an arrow serves the function of the wheel (J. Mooney 1982:434), suggesting that the wheel itself is not a crucial motif in this story incident.

The Sequoyah Syllabary and Cultural Revitalization

Theda Perdue

In 1821, Sequoyah, who spoke only Cherokee and wrote no language, accomplished an amazing feat: he invented a system for writing his native tongue. At a time when most Americans retained vivid memories of war with the Shawnees and Creeks, Sequoyah's achievement seemed to set the Cherokees apart. Cherokee leaders actively promoted this view and took great care to distance themselves from other native peoples. As Shawnees, Senecas, Creeks, and others attempted to control and direct the enormous changes that engulfed them through nativistic revitalization movements, the Cherokees turned to acculturation and embraced the United States government's "civilization" program. Although many Cherokees lagged behind their nation's leaders in transforming their values, practices, and beliefs, there was little overt opposition to "civilization." The enthusiastic response and rapid adoption of literacy seemed to signal an endorsement of "civilization" by most Cherokees, who exhibited scant appreciation of other accouterments. A reconsideration of the development and adoption of the Cherokee syllabary, however, suggests that the Cherokee elite and subsequent historians may have misinterpreted literacy's appeal. Many Cherokees seem to have regarded Sequoyah as a kind of prophet, a person with unusual spiritual power, and a nativistic rather than an imitative impulse may have prompted their acceptance of his syllabary. Such a reinterpretation places Cherokee literacy within the context of other early nineteenth-century native revitalization movements. Furthermore, it provides insight into the survival and modern use of the Sequoyah syllabary.

The key to understanding Cherokee literacy lies in the circumstances surrounding Sequoyah's invention of a syllabary for writing the language. Sequoyah, who was born about 1770, began work on the syllabary about 1809. The War of 1812, in which he and other Cherokees fought for the United States, interrupted his efforts. After the war he became involved in treaty negotiations that culminated in a land cession, and in 1818 he and other displaced Cherokees left their kinsmen and moved west of the Mississippi River, where he resumed his work. In 1821 he abandoned earlier attempts to design a character for each word and instead designed a symbol for each syllable; the symbols could then be combined to make words. After he adopted this method, Sequoyah reportedly completed the eighty-six-symbol syllabary (later reduced to eighty-five) in about one month. After introducing the system in the West, Sequoyah traveled in 1822 or 1823 to his old homeland in the East, where the vast majority of Cherokees still lived, to teach it to the people there. In 1824 the Eastern Cherokee Council honored Sequoyah with a medal (Foreman 1938).

The Sequoyah syllabary, which could be mastered quickly by native speakers, was an immediate success. In April 1832, Elias Boudinot, editor of the bilingual *Cherokee Phoenix,* reported to the *American Annals of Education* that "it spread through the nation in a manner unprecedented. Reading and writing very soon became common, for within a few months after its introduction, there were Cherokees in various parts of the nation who could use the '*talking leaf.*' " Boudinot estimated that by 1830 "upwards of one half of the adult males could read and write in their own language" (Perdue 1983:58). According to the 1835 census, 43 percent of Cherokee households had members who could read the Sequoyah syllabary, an amazing literacy rate after only a decade of use (Indian Affairs 1835). Boudinot predicted that "it will be but a few years before reading and writing will be universal among them." The subsequent tragedy of forced removal to the West and a bitter civil war made this an elusive goal.

According to many of his contemporaries, Sequoyah's invention of a system for writing the Cherokee language ushered in the golden age of Cherokee "civilization." Boudinot described Sequoyah in the *American Annals of Education* (April 1, 1832) as a "great benefactor of the Cherokees, who, by his inventive powers, has raised them to an elevation unattained by any other Indian nation, and made them a reading and intellectual people." Principal Chief John Ross wrote to Sequoyah in English on January 12, 1832, that his accomplishment would "serve as an index for the aboriginal tribes, or nations, similarly to advance in science and respectability" (Moulton 1985, 1:234–35). Historians have accepted the Cherokee leaders' assessment of Sequoyah and his invention. Grant Foreman (1930:46, 1938:81) contended that the syllabary "contributed more than any other factor to the advanced position which the Cherokees occupied among the tribes." More recently, linguist Willard Walker (1975:193) described Sequoyah's achievement as "one of the most remarkable *tours de force* in American history."

The invention of the syllabary coincided with a broader transformation of Cherokee culture and society in response to the ravages of war and depletion of game in the late eighteenth century. In the early nineteenth century the Cherokee Nation abolished blood revenge, began to record their laws, established a police force to apprehend offenders and courts to try them, created a central government with a bicameral legislature, wrote a republican constitution, and took conflicts with their neighbors to the United States Supreme Court. An elite whose wealth rested on commercial agriculture and trade dominated political life and lived like southern planters. The Cherokees welcomed missionaries, who built a system of schools few southern communities could rival, and church membership approximated that in the white South. In 1828 the Cherokees bought a printing press and began a newspaper. Sequoyah's accomplishment thus came in the midst of a cultural transformation that apparently sought acculturation rather than revitalization.

Scholars of Cherokee history have most frequently used the acculturation model to describe Cherokee culture change (Malone 1956). According to this view the Cherokees retained some of their traditions but adopted many aspects of the dominant culture. Grace Steele Woodward (1963:3) claimed that "the Cherokee tribe of Indians reached a higher peak of civilization than any other North American Indian tribe"; and William G. McLoughlin (1984b:2) suggested that "they provided a model both to the leaders of other Indian nations and to the missionaries. By the 1820s they had become, in the missionaries' eyes, 'the most civilized tribe in America.' " Cherokee leaders provided ample evidence on which these scholars could base their interpretations. In the columns of the *Cherokee Phoenix,* Boudinot carefully distinguished the Cherokees from the "American Arabs" of the plains, perpetrators of "massacres" and other "atrocities." He pointed out that "the situation of the Cherokees is very different from the few [native] remnants in the northern states" and responded to descriptions of "the degraded state of our neighbor Creeks, and their rapid decline" by protesting "against associating the Cherokees with them under the general name of 'Southern Indians'" (*Cherokee Phoenix*, September 30, 1829, January 6, 1830, July 21, 1828).

McLoughlin (1986), however, also suggested that the Cherokees' cultural transformation may best be understood as a syncretic process in which they borrowed from Anglo-Americans while retaining elements of their own culture in order to create new ways of organizing their lives and understanding the world. McLoughlin's description of this process approaches Anthony F. C. Wallace's classic definition of revitalization as "a deliberate, organized, conscious effort by members of a society to construct a more satisfying culture" (1956:164). The leadership of other contemporary revitalization movements, however, came from religious figures who experienced visions, claimed special knowledge, and extolled the virtues of Indian ways over white ones. The Cherokees had prophets, but their teachings lacked much of the religious fervor found elsewhere. The Cherokees focused on practical political issues rather than on esoteric spiritual ones. The "ghost dance" movement of 1811–13 had religious overtones, but it centered on politics (McLoughlin 1984a). The opposition to Christianity that arose a decade later stemmed primarily from the missionaries' injunction against converts entering the council house where political deliberations took place (Perdue 1982). In both cases the movements attracted relatively few followers, and Cherokee culture change remained firmly in the hands of acculturationists. Even if we consider nineteenth-century Cherokee "civilization" to be revitalization, the movement still bears little resemblance to contemporary movements. The Cherokees did not invoke native culture, even a radically altered culture—instead, they appeared to abandon it.

The Cherokees' adoption of Sequoyah's writing system has been understood in terms of the nation's move toward "civilization"; that is, toward commercial agriculture, republican government, Christianity, and English education. If this had been the case, widespread literacy would have signaled acceptance of the "civilization" program by the majority of Cherokees, and their leaders would have stood at the forefront of the movement. In the early nineteenth century, however, considerable apathy and even hostility to "civilization" was present among the Cherokees. Understandably reluctant to admit the recalcitrance of many of their citizens, Cherokee leaders and sympathetic missionaries only rarely alluded to the deep cultural divisions in Cherokee society. In the heat of the removal debate, however, Boudinot referred to the condition of the mass of Cherokees as a "dreary waste" among whom he saw nothing to "encourage a philanthropist" (Perdue 1983:223). The Cherokee removal roll reveals a people who had adopted the necessary skills to survive but apparently had not become either "assimilationist or deculturated" (McLoughlin 1984a:238). Most practiced subsistence-level agriculture and demonstrated little enthusiasm for the acquisitive, individualistic value system endorsed by their leaders. Unlike their unchurched white neighbors, the overwhelming majority of Cherokees who resisted the altar call subscribed to non-Christian religious beliefs. The single aspect of Cherokee culture change for which we can document extensive grass-roots support is adoption of the syllabary. The masses, in fact, embraced Sequoyah's syllabary far more readily than did the official leadership of the nation. What does this mean?

The invention of the syllabary impressed those who were culturally European as an extraordinary technological and intellectual achievement. As such, it appeared to have little in common with the nativistic revitalization movements so widespread in early nineteenth-century America. Although these movements came to have political, social, and even technological components, their leaders asserted a spiritual authority and their mass appeal lay largely in their religious imperative. By contrast, Cherokee leadership rested with market-oriented planters and businessmen like Chief John Ross and Christian intellectuals like Elias Boudinot. No Cherokee prophet appealed to the people to create a new but uniquely Cherokee culture, and many Cherokees were reluctant to adopt a hollow, cold "civilization" that lacked a spiritual dimension. The Cherokees' enthusiasm for the Sequoyah syllabary may reflect their need to fill a spiritual vacuum. The Cherokee masses may have understood the syllabary not as an invention that was the result of years of labor but as the product of visions and spiritual forces beyond human comprehension or control.

Sequoyah apparently did not share this view, but his own account of the invention gives considerable insight into how other people viewed it. In 1827, the literary scholar Samuel Lorenzo Knapp met Sequoyah in Washington, D.C. The interview conducted at that time was published in Knapp's *Lectures on American Literature, with Remarks on Some Passages of American History.* Elias Boudinot reprinted the lecture in the *Cherokee Phoenix* (July 29, 1829) and used it as the basis for his article "Invention of a New Alphabet" (Perdue 1983:48–58). Sequoyah reportedly told Knapp that his interest in developing a system for writing Cherokee stemmed from the capture of a white soldier during a late eighteenth-century campaign. The Cherokee war party of which Sequoyah was a member discovered a letter in the soldier's possession, and this discovery prompted a discussion of literacy. Knapp recorded Sequoyah's recollection: "In some deliberations on this subject, the question arose among them, whether this mysterious power of *the talking leaf,* was the gift of the Great Spirit to the white man, or the discovery of the white man himself? Most of his companions were of the former opinion, while he as strenuously maintained the latter" (Perdue 1983:51). In other words, most Cherokees believed that writing was spiritual rather than mechanical, a gift of the gods rather than a creation of man.

Sequoyah's conviction that writing was a human invention led him to attempt to commit his own language to written form. Most of his fellow Cherokees, however, continued to view literacy as mystical, even occult, and they came to regard Sequoyah with considerable suspicion. Knapp reported: "His former companions passed his wigwam without entering it, and mentioned his name as one who was practising improper spells, for notoriety or mischievous purposes; and he seems to think that he should have been hardly dealt with [probably convicted of witchcraft], if his docile and unambitious disposition had not been so generally acknowledged by his tribe" (Perdue 1983:55).

When Sequoyah finally perfected his syllabary, he presented it to an assembled group of Cherokees using his daughter to demonstrate how Cherokees could communicate. People suspected that this was a trick, and so, according to Knapp, "Sequoyah then proposed, that the tribe should select several youths from among their brightest young men, that he might communicate the mystery to them" (Perdue 1983:55). In order to gain acceptance for his syllabary, Sequoyah was now appealing to his people in terms they understood and accepted: he would "communicate the mystery to them." The people agreed to the plan, but "there was some lurking suspicion of necromancy in the whole business," and they "watched the youths for several months with anxiety" (Perdue 1983:55). When the young men at last demonstrated their competence in reading and writing the Cherokee language, the Cherokees held a feast in Sequoyah's honor. According to Knapp, "His countrymen were proud of his talents, and held him in reverence as one favored by the Great Spirit" (Perdue 1983:56). The Cherokees regarded the development of the syllabary as evidence of their spiritual worth, and their rapid mastery of it was an affirmation of themselves as a people.

The highly acculturated Cherokee elite, who had centralized the government, converted to Christianity, learned English, bought slaves, and prospered from commercial agriculture, did not at first accept Sequoyah's syllabary. These Cherokees, in fact, were oblivious to the syllabary's existence until many others had already become literate. Elias Boudinot, who had been educated in New England, was totally unaware of Sequoyah until 1823 when Principal Chief John Ross pointed out Sequoyah's cabin and referred to his "foolish undertaking." Boudinot wrote: "I thought no more of Sequoyah and his alphabet, until a portion of the Cherokees had *actually* become a reading people. The first evidence I received of the existence of the alphabet, was at a General Council held in New Echota in 1824, when I saw a number of the Cherokees reading and writing in their own language, and in the new characters invented by one of their untutored citizens" (Perdue 1983:54–55).

Highly acculturated Cherokees such as Boudinot had difficulty accepting a system of writing devised by an illiterate native speaker. Instead they tended to favor the orthography of John Pickering, a noted philologist whom a Protestant missionary society had employed to develop a system for writing native languages and translating the Bible. The vast majority of Cherokees, however, would have nothing to do with Pickering's grammar. In July 1827, Samuel Austin Worcester, an unusually perceptive and sensitive white missionary, wrote in the *Boston Missionary Herald:* "Whether or not the perception of the Cherokees is correct, in regard to the superiority of their own alphabet for their own use, that impression they have, and it is not easy to be eradicated. It would be a vain attempt to persuade them to relinquish their own method of writing." He warned the promoters of Pickering's system that "if books are printed in Guess's [Sequoyah's] character, they will be read; if in any other, they will lie useless." Consequently, Worcester, Boudinot, Ross, and others accepted the Sequoyah syllabary and enlisted it in the cultural transformation of the Cherokees. In 1828, under Boudinot's editorship, the Cherokee Nation began to publish a newspaper, the *Cherokee Phoenix,* in both English and the Sequoyah syllabary. Cherokee national laws were published in both languages, and Boudinot and Worcester collaborated on the translation of the Bible and Christian hymns. The syllabary was without doubt a major factor in the early nineteenth-century political regeneration of the Cherokees that led to their valiant but unsuccessful resistance to removal west of the Mississippi.

And while the Sequoyah syllabary may have been an agent of acculturation for some Cherokees, others who adopted the syllabary shunned certain aspects of Anglo-American culture. Sequoyah himself projected the image of a relatively traditional Cherokee both in his Charles Bird King portrait and in the following description given by Ethan Allen Hitchcock in 1841: "He has an extremely interesting, intelligent countenance, full of cheerful animation with an evident vein of good humor— may be 55 or 60 years of age—habitually wears a shawl turban and dresses rudely." Hitchcock also noted that "though the missionaries in the Country have been successful in converting many Cherokees to Christianity by the aid of the invention of Cherokee writing, they have failed to make an impression upon the inventor, who is not friendly to their course" (Foreman 1930:241–44). Learning to read and write did not transform a Cherokee into a white man. New forms of discourse and the extension of abstractions did not necessarily compromise traditional Cherokee values and beliefs; in some cases the syllabary actually enhanced them. For example, the syllabary enabled Cherokees who might otherwise have become estranged from one another because of distance to communicate and maintain the sense of community so important in traditional society.

Willard Walker suggested that in order for a nonliterate people to learn to read and write, they must accept the innovators, recognize the usefulness of literacy, and accept both the writing system and its literature (1969:148–49). The Cherokees accepted Sequoyah because they interpreted his achievement in traditional, spiritual terms. But the result of his accomplishment—writing—had no traditional basis in Cherokee life, and for it to become widespread, people needed to find it useful and the literature it produced satisfying. In the decade following the syllabary's introduction in the East, a significant proportion of Cherokees apparently found no good use for writing. In 1835, 39 percent of Cherokee households contained no literate members. While they may have appreciated and respected Sequoyah, these people saw no compelling reason to learn his syllabary. Perhaps they had little interest in the newspaper or national laws and no distant relatives.

As more Cherokees learned English, however, and English became the standard language for conducting the Cherokee Nation's political affairs, traditionalists found an important use for the syllabary that did not involve a new form of discourse. It became a means to preserve traditional religious knowledge. In fact, perhaps the largest surviving body of material in the Sequoyah syllabary pertains to traditional religion. Shamans carefully recorded sacred formulas as they remembered them. Swimmer, an eastern Cherokee shaman who died in 1899, committed his formulas to writing in the only language he knew—Cherokee. No longer trusting his memory, and concerned that the younger generation did not exhibit sufficient interest in the old ways, Swimmer meticulously recorded his knowledge, including sacred words whose meanings he either did not know or declined to translate. The anthropologist James Mooney expressed his "astonishment" at discovering Swimmer's notebook in the late nineteenth century (1886:312). Mooney clearly did not expect a Cherokee shaman to record on paper with pen and ink his prescriptions for curing illness, hunting bear, and solving marital problems. Writing, after all, was part of the European cultural heritage. Yet Cherokees understood the syllabary in their own terms. The syllabary, a product of years of solitary struggle, had spiritual significance, and its adoption affirmed a Cherokee worldview. Recording sacred formulas was an eminently appropriate use for it.

In 1971, Traveler Bird, a descendant of Sequoyah, published an account of the Cherokee writing system that alleged a more ancient and spiritual origin than most Cherokees and modern scholars accept. He claimed that missionaries in collusion with the Cherokee elite fabricated the story of his ancestor's invention of the syllabary and appropriated a version of an ancient writing system for their own nefarious ends—in particular, "civilization" and Christianization. Traveler Bird's account does not stand up to scrutiny in the Western academic tradition (Fogelson 1974), but he captured the essence of the syllabary's popular appeal. The syllabary connected the Cherokees to the past—literally, in Traveler Bird's account, to the time before white men arrived, but also to a tradition that was not so mechanistic. The syllabary represented a revelation, a vision, a spiritual experience in a world in which such occurrences no longer seemed to have much significance. Their interpretation of the syllabary in spiritual terms joined Cherokees to their contemporary native peoples in a way that is not otherwise apparent, and the popular response to Sequoyah and his syllabary reveals a nativistic spiritual dimension to Cherokee culture change. Furthermore, this interpretation of writing enabled them to view literacy in the Cherokee language as a part of native knowledge, not as a repudiation of their own culture and a step toward "civilization." Although contact with Euro-Americans may have inspired Sequoyah, the process by which most Cherokees believed he acquired the ability to read and write was not new. Understood in traditional terms, the syllabary gave the Cherokees an impetus to revitalize their own culture while adapting to changed circumstances: it linked their past to the future.

In the last half of the twentieth century the Sequoyah syllabary has continued to serve the same function in many Cherokee communities. Walker observed that "Cherokees associate literacy with knowledge, and knowledge is prerequisite to the full acceptance of an individual as a mature responsible member of the Cherokee community." Many Cherokees have learned to read their own language in their thirties, in church. They use Cherokee primarily for "participation in religious activities and the practice of Indian medicine" (1969:151). Written Cherokee thus continues to have a mystical and spiritual appeal that points scholars to its origin and forecasts its survival.

Ethnoarchaeology of the Lamar Peoples

John H. Moore

Southeastern archaeologists have something to gain by collaborating with ethnologists such as myself, and I hope to convince them of that in this essay. First I will make some general remarks about ethnographic analogy, arguing from a theoretical perspective that the modern Creeks are the most appropriate ethnographic source for interpreting the Lamar peoples, the Creeks' presumed ancestors, who lived in the Southeast at the time of Columbus (Fairbanks 1952; Howard 1968; Walthall 1980:271; M. Williams and Shapiro 1990:3). In my discussion I will criticize some current practices of archaeologists in applying ethnography to their work and suggest guidelines that might help to structure a more valid, collaborative approach. After this introduction I will offer two modest but colorful examples of recent practices of Oklahoma Creeks and Seminoles that might be relevant in the interpretation of the culture of the Lamar peoples.

I agree with archaeologists that one important function of ethnology is to provide ethnographic illustrations that will assist in interpreting archaeological evidence. Unfortunately, much published ethnography is not suitable for these purposes because too many ethnologists have an agenda that is self-contained and inconsiderate of the needs of archaeologists. Many recent ethnographic monographs written from a structuralist or deconstructive perspective contain very little that would help an archaeologist; for example, methods of building houses, laying out a new village, making tools, or digging graves.

Of course, ethnographic analogy is undertaken for different purposes, and these require different kinds of facts. Two of these purposes I find particularly interesting. First, analogy is sometimes used to reconstruct cultural universals. All the known occurrences of an archaeological phenomenon, such as a pit house, are toted up to find universal correlations with such variables as climate or environment (Gilman 1987). This is the approach encouraged by the Human Relations Area Files.

A second, more modest, purpose is served, however, when analogy is used merely to fill the gaps of knowledge for a particular site or type of site. Archaeologists, like everyone else, want to know what kind of behavior might have produced an archaeological feature and how that behavior might be related to other kinds of behavior suggested by the findings at the same site. It is this more modest and explicitly function-alist purpose of ethnographic analogy that I will primarily address in this essay with my examples and my criticisms.

It seems to me that archaeologists sometimes misuse or misunder-stand the ethnographic literature. So, before I suggest some guidelines for ethnographic analogy, let me first criticize two current practices that are particularly troublesome from an ethnological perspective. Since I am hoping to encourage cooperation and collaboration with south-eastern archaeologists, it may be politic to direct my criticisms at the archaeologists of other geographical areas as much as I can. So let me first select an example from my friend and colleague at Oklahoma, Paul Minnis, and criticize the practice of taking ethnographic analogies out of their cultural contexts.

In explaining behavior in times of famine in the American Southwest, Minnis points to an example from the Tonga of Africa, who under simi-lar conditions hid food from their neighbors and ate in the seclusion of their individual homes (Minnis 1985:30–33). He hypothesizes that the southwestern Indians may have done the same, thereby explaining cer-tain features of their architecture. What is missing from this analogy is specifically who these neighbors might have been, both in the Southwest and among the Tonga.

In a unilocal society such as those found in the Southwest, people live next door either to their own siblings or to the siblings of their spouse. Sibships are universally groups that share food and pool resources, and it seems unlikely that a person would hide food from a sibling, no matter how acute the famine. Although the Tonga analogy might be correct, we need more information about who their neighbors were before we can use it. That is, the burden on Minnis must be to reconstruct the analogy in its entirety, showing that the kinship and residence patterns were the same in Africa as in the Southwest.

Another current problem in ethnographic analogy has resulted, in my opinion, from the forays of scholars such as Richard Gould and Lewis Binford into ethnographic fieldwork, an enterprise that has been labeled "ethnoarchaeology" (Gould 1980; L. Binford 1978). While I understand the frustrations of archaeologists who are dissatisfied with published ethnographies and decide to conduct their own fieldwork, it seems that they often do so by reference to distorted or at least redefined ethnographic concepts. Binford, for example, uses the term *kinship* to describe the extent of social solidarity among hunting and gathering peoples (L. Binford 1992). That is, he points out that some societies showed cooperation among members of extended families, and thus had "good kinship," while others presumably had "bad kinship." Although I know what he means, this nonstandard use of the word *kinship* creates a great deal of confusion between ethnologists and archaeologists.

To pick an example from the Southeast, although I hate to do so, the definition of *moiety* in archaeological scholarship has been extended far beyond its normal range in ethnology. For ethnologists, the term *moiety* is strictly sociological and refers to a societal population divided in half by reference to some contrasting set of symbols, like sun and moon, or summer and winter, or land and sea. In Southeastern prehistory, however, the term has been extended to include not only the population but the symbols themselves, the relevant decorative art, and even the physical orientation of a site or of the architectural features (Knight 1986, 1990). By contrast, most ethnologists would refer to these features as "dualistic" or, perhaps, "polarized." Here again, I know what the author means, but the use of *moiety* in this manner creates a barrier of misunderstanding between archaeologists and ethnologists.

With these critical comments as background, then, I turn now to a few guidelines for ethnographic analogy. In my review of the archaeological literature (admittedly superficial) I found no explicit, generally agreed-on rules for selecting ethnographic examples for analogy. In fact, I was amazed to see that examples of behavior that do not appear in the ethnographic literature at all are sometimes selected. That is, archaeologists sometimes explain an archaeological phenomenon by reference to ethnographic behavior that is completely undocumented. For example, Michael Glassow has stated that spears, darts, and atlatls are associated with a hunting-collecting mode of production and bows and arrows are associated with agriculture, without providing any ethnographic survey to support this clearly erroneous generalization (Glassow 1972:298–99). As another example, Martin, Plog, and Gorman have suggested that lithic variability at an archaeological site can be explained in terms of personal styles adopted to assert ownership of the kill, once again without citing an ethnographic example of this practice (Martin and Plog 1973:217–18).

In view of these examples, let me make a modest and self-interested suggestion here, in the form of a first guideline or scholarly canon, simply that:

1. The postulated activities of culture-bearers at some particular site must necessarily fall somewhere within the spectrum of known human behavior. After more than a hundred years of ethnographic fieldwork, a huge range of possibilities exists, and it should be unnecessary for an archaeologist to reconstruct postulated behavior based entirely on a theoretical rather than an empirical basis, except as a last resort. I realize, of course, that this canon flies in the face of the Binfords' assertion that there is a "high probability that cultural forms existed in the past for which we have no ethnographic examples" (S. Binford and Binford 1968:13). But it seems to me that this attitude invites a certain laziness on the part of archaeologists who don't want to read ethnography, and it preapproves the kind of bizarre theories cited above. The kind of discipline imposed by the requirement of ethnographic analogy provides the same kind of charter for success as that provided by the principle of uniformitarianism in geology.

As a second and related canon for ethnographic analogy, let me suggest that:

2. Different analogies chosen to explain the same site should be functionally consistent with one another. That is, it seems counterproductive to select, for example, the Tonga to explain one feature of a site and the Mundurucu to explain another. Doing this risks creating a contradictory picture of events, because each analogy chosen must necessarily imply a larger, distinctive cultural context. For example, one should not choose one bit of behavior that fits within a system of strongly agnatic clans and another that is a product of a matrifocal household; these institutions clearly are not likely to occur within the same society. One should not create literally monstrous societies to explain puzzling archaeological features.

I have said that ethnographic analogies should be selected from real examples that are consistent with one another. How, then, does one select the most appropriate analogy from the range of documented possibilities? For this let me suggest a third canon, based on an inversion of Galton's Problem, which we can call Galton's Observation. As everyone knows, Galton pointed out that in sampling human societies for correlations, one has to avoid including contiguous or near-contiguous societies, which are similar only because traits have diffused from one to the other. For example, in investigating the universal functions of age-set systems, one should include the Arapahoes *or* the Atsinas, but not both, because they are historically and geographically connected.

But for the same reasons, in selecting societies for analogy one could argue that the nearest geographical neighbors are not the worst but the best choices. That is, if one must choose between the Choctaws and the Tongas in selecting ethnographic analogies for the Creeks, then clearly the Choctaws are the better choice. This criterion is implicitly recognized by many archaeologists and ethnohistorians, and I only wish to make it explicit here as a third canon:

3. Other things being equal, the most appropriate ethnographic analogies are those closest in space and time to the culture being interpreted. It is not necessarily the case that the actual descendants of a society are the best sources for ethnographic analogy. For example, I have asserted elsewhere that to understand the Cheyennes in their Great Lakes period, about 1680, it is more appropriate to use the nineteenth-century Chippewas, who occupied the same area at a later time, than the nineteenth-century Cheyennes, who by that time had become pastoral buffalo hunters. But in the case of the Lamar peoples, no current occupants of the area can serve as good analogues.

In such a situation I would suggest a fourth and final canon, which is also based on a long-respected practice among archaeologists, the direct-historical method. Making the canon explicit, I suggest that:

4. Other things being equal, the most appropriate source for ethnographic analogy is the descendants of the society being investigated. In this case, I am not sure that it is still proper to use the term *analogy,* since we may be dealing not with an analogue but with an identical or cognate practice. So perhaps the word *residue,* which entered the anthropological literature through Edward Tylor and Vilfredo Pareto, might be more appropriate to describe a practice retained through time. Using the term *residue* also calls to mind the excellent theoretical discussions by Tylor and Pareto about transformations among form, function, and ideology, which are still of great value (Tylor 1913; Pareto 1980). The point of reviewing all these canons, of course, is to argue, on a theoretical basis, that the modern Creeks and Seminoles of Oklahoma are the best place to begin when looking for cultural practices that will help us understand the artifacts of their ancestors, the Lamar people in particular.

BELLS, HORNS, TRUMPETS, AND CONCHS

Let me now drop from theory to the ethnographic grass roots and present some observations that support the appropriateness of looking at modern Creeks to understand Lamar archaeology. To my mind, the most important use of Creek ethnography as analogy, ultimately, will be to help in understanding Lamar political structure, but that is a complicated problem. To stay within the constraints of this essay, I instead call attention to two rather colorful "residues" in modern Mvskoke life, conch trumpets and indoor burials. Although my fieldwork among them began about 1981, I did not begin a comprehensive survey of Creek communities until 1985, when I began to construct generalizations about current Mvskoke practices. I have visited eight of the active Creek and Seminole stomp grounds and all but three of the fifty-one native Mvskoke churches. Formally and informally, I have talked to hundreds of Creek traditionalists about these matters.

For a long time I avoided attending the Mvskoke Christian churches, under the mistaken notion that their congregations represented the more acculturated sector of the population. Such notions quickly disappeared, however, on my first Sunday at the Prairie Springs Indian Baptist Church near Okemah, Oklahoma, in 1985 when the service was called to order by a long, low drone from a trumpet somewhere in the back of the church, a practice unknown in local non-Indian churches. After the service I asked a deacon where the sound had come from, and he showed me a heavy piece of iron, which he called a *kiboje*. Although he didn't know what it was called in English, he said it was part of a wagon. (I later identified the piece as a wheel hub; see Figure 1.) When I asked the deacon how long the church had used this artifact, he answered that

Fig. 1. Used as a trumpet in a modern Creek Indian Methodist church, a wheel hub from horse-drawn wagon.

they had used it ever since their conch trumpet had been dropped and broken, when he was a child. I asked where the conch had come from, and he said it had been brought from Alabama.

In my survey of churches over the next several years I discovered five other churches that had wheel hub trumpets and two that still maintained their original conch trumpets (Figure 2). The surviving shell trumpets seem to be made from the Florida horse conch (*Pleuroploca gigantea*), one of the species identified by Jerald T. Milanich from Lamar sites (Abbott 1962:85; Milanich 1979:86). All the elders I interviewed told the same story: many of the churches had originally had conch trumpets, and the wheel hubs had been substituted when the conchs were broken because they sounded like conchs when they were blown. Cow horns and ear trumpets were less-preferred substitutes for conchs because they produced a different, higher-pitched sound (Figure 3).

The modern trend among Indian churches, however, is to retire all the trumpets and horns as the churches acquire bells and bell towers (Figure 4). Although some churches went directly from conch to horn or

Fig. 2. Conch trumpet and cow horn currently used in a Creek Indian Baptist church.

Fig. 3. Ear trumpet and cow horn currently used as trumpets to signal the beginning of church services in a Creek Indian Baptist church.

Fig. 4. Bell tower and belfry in use in a Creek Indian Baptist church.

Fig. 5. Deacons' sticks hanging on a wall of a Creek Indian Baptist church. These sticks are similar to the sticks used by official criers at traditional stomp grounds.

wheel hub to bell, the general historical progression of the use of these instruments seems to be (1) conch trumpet (2) to wheel hub trumpet (3) to cow horn (4) to bell. This progression is vulnerable, I believe, to a theoretical analysis that considers the interplay among form, function, and ideology, but I will not attempt that here. The original purpose of all these instruments, according to elders, was to summon the membership, who were scattered for individual prayer in the woods around the church building.

A developing ethnographic literature shows that the Mvskoke churches are not very "Christian" by European standards, and in fact are merely translations into a Christian idiom of the activities of the traditional stomp grounds, which are in turn more directly related to the ceremonial sites of the Lamar peoples. So the obvious question concerning conch trumpets is whether such trumpets have the same function in the stomp grounds. If so, they might be extrapolated further back to the Lamar period. But the ethnographic answer at present seems to be that no trumpets of any kind have been used at stomp grounds within the memories of modern elders. At the grounds, there is no need to summon anyone from afar, since the camp houses are in sight of one another, and any summoning necessary is done by official criers who tour the arbors carrying decorated staffs of office (Figure 5).

When the Creeks and Seminoles moved to Oklahoma, only a few were Christians, and there were no organized congregations. If conch shells were brought along, they must have been brought by the people who conducted ceremonies at the stomp grounds, not by pastors and deacons. In the late 1800s, however, many of the grounds were transformed into native churches, often with their ceremonial leadership intact, and so the possibility exists that conchs previously used in the traditional ceremonies were adapted for church use. Neither of the two surviving conch trumpets shows any indication of carving or decoration that might imply that it was once used for traditional ceremonies. The "deacon sticks" used in the churches, however, have clan markings on the handle and other symbols identical to those on the staffs of office used at the stomp grounds.

Although Mvskoke elders unanimously state that conch trumpets were never used at the stomp grounds, they are equally unanimous in relating that *all* the grounds originally had conch dippers or cups for taking black drink, which has been well reported in the ethnographic literature (Howard 1968:74–76). As far as I know, these original conch dippers were either buried with past religious leaders or else are now maintained exclusively as relics, most often in broken pieces. Some of them are decorated, but these may be archaeological artifacts brought from the Southeast.

Archaeological reports of Lamar sites mention conchs only as cups or dippers, not as trumpets (Milanich 1979), but farther south, in Mexico and elsewhere in Middle America, conch trumpets were in use for hundreds of years before Lamar times (Bushnell 1965:102; Kerr 1990:278, 307; de Sahagun 1979:35). Might not some of the Lamar conchs also have been used as trumpets? As artifacts, perhaps the only difference between a conch cup and a conch trumpet is that the spiral tip has been sawed off to make a mouthpiece, a detail that might be missed in analyzing fragments.

BURIALS, PROXIMITY, AND THE KINSHIP SYSTEM

It did not occur to me to ask modern Mvskokes about indoor burials until after a personal conversation with Jim Hatch in 1988. In my survey of churches I had become aware that Indian Christians constructed rather unique cemeteries near their churches, and I was also aware that in the nineteenth and early twentieth centuries many Creeks were buried in family plots rather than in cemeteries. But I was completely unprepared for what happened in the summer of 1992, when I discovered that traditional Creeks still bury people inside their houses.

Indoor burial, as Ethan Allen Hitchcock discovered in 1842, is not very obvious (Hitchcock 1930:112). There is no tombstone or marker; one has to be told that the grave is there. Sensitive to the criticisms of white people and of Christian Indians, traditional Creeks are reluctant to discuss these matters. But the recommended patterns of burial can be discovered by tactful interviews, and the reasons for the different patterns are still a matter of hot debate among Creeks of different religious persuasions.

In my interviews, the first question I asked concerned the attitudes of survivors toward the ghost of the person buried in the home, since Creeks are notoriously wary of the ghosts of recently departed people. The answer to this is simply that the family has no reason to fear the ghost of a loved one, and in fact the ghost will defend the family against outsiders. Also, the grave and the ghost in the house are said to impart

Fig. 6. Modern Creek Indian graveyard near a rural Baptist church.

a sobriety and seriousness to family life, as if the departed person were still there. While one might misbehave somewhere in public, one is less likely to misbehave on the grave of one's grandmother or dead son. These interior graves are constant reminders of the importance of family life and the obligation to one's kin. Moreover, we can confirm both from modern practice and from published ethnography that the people buried in a house are in fact the former residents of that house.

Modern Christian Creeks bury their dead almost shoulder to shoulder in graveyards near the church building, in the order of their death, and are consequently criticized by traditionalists for burying people next to strangers (Figure 6). In response, Christians say that all members of a congregation are brother and sister to one another, and so all members are at rest as a family in Christ. Traditionalists also criticize the proximity of church to graveyard and say that the nearness of the dead pollutes the Christian services. The traditionalists themselves normally do not bury their dead near the stomp grounds, as might be expected, and in fact prefer to be buried in a Christian cemetery if burial at home or in a family plot is impossible.

Certain practical problems about burial at home have discouraged the practice in recent decades. Modern homes are built on a concrete slab, which precludes burial indoors. In such cases, the burial can be made in a floorless shed or outbuilding, or even in the barn or garage. Nowadays it is infants and old people who most often are buried at home.

The unique grave houses built by Creeks and Seminoles over their graves, both in church cemeteries and in family plots, are explained as a response to the necessity of burying people outside. When houses became more permanent in Indian Territory and had wooden floors, people became reluctant to tear up the floor to bury a person. Instead, little houses were built over the outside graves "to keep the rain off their faces." A rationale offered for indoor burials is that the family did not want the deceased "to be lonesome and cold."

Modern burials, just like those described in the Lamar archaeological reports (Hatch 1975), tend to be cosmologically oriented, although there is some contradiction in the rationales offered by modern Creeks. The dead are buried lying face-up, usually with the head to the west, propped up on a pillow so that the deceased can see the sunrise or the Holy Land or Jesus at the Second Coming. Some burials are with the head to the east, but the rationale for the orientation is the same. Others rationalize a burial with the head to the east as enabling the deceased to see westward "down the road to eternity." The point is that these opposite orientations are both rationalized in the same manner.

Hatch has raised some concerns about the composition of burial groups found in Lamar households (Hatch 1975). Why, for example, is there so frequently only one senior male buried in the house structure? The answer, I propose, is based both on the pattern of ghost beliefs and on the logic of matrilocal rules of residence.

In the first place, modern Creeks say that a widow or widower has no reason to fear the ghost of a departed spouse. But Creeks are less emphatic about whether a son or daughter might have reason to be concerned. And we should recall that in a matrilineal system the father and his children belong to different clans, and that the close relationship is usually between children and mother's brother, not children and father. Friction is common between a man and his children.

If the mother of a family dies and is buried in the house, her husband is unafraid because he continues to feel love and affection for her, and the children are likewise unafraid of her ghost because they represent the same clan and are, in addition, her heirs. If the widower is young and has children to raise, by traditional practice a real or classificatory sister of his wife might be supplied by her clan and family to replace her as wife. So the domestic system continues much as before, except with the mother interred in the house and replaced by a clanswoman.

But if the father dies, there are different consequences. First of all, if the widow is young, the father's clan might supply a substitute father for her children under the levirate. But if the deceased father is older and the children are grown, and especially if his wife predeceased him, some familial stress is created. In a matrilocal society, the sons have married out and the only people left at home are the daughters and their spouses, if any. The intermarried sons-in-law, especially, might be in different clans and consequently in situations of social and ceremonial friction with one another and with the ghost of their deceased father-in-law. But the situation can be simplified for the younger generation if they move to a different house, away from the grave and ghost of the father. Swan, an early traveler, speaking in 1791, confirmed this kind of reasoning when he said, "If the deceased has been a man of eminent character, the family immediately remove from the house in which he is buried, and erect a new one, with a belief that where the bones of their dead are deposited, the place is always attended by 'goblins and chimeras dire'" (Schoolcraft 1857:270).

In sum, while the death of the mother does not create any ritual or sociological confusion, the death of a father does, and it triggers the movement of the survivors to a different house. Other factors contributing to a regular change of residence and to this particular domestic cycle in Lamar times might also include the need to find fertile fields in a system of shifting cultivation and the fact that a house simply wears out after a time. These material facts can easily be synchronized with biological facts by a cultural tradition of moving out of a house after the father is buried there.

Since Lamar times the Mvskoke people have undergone major cultural changes. They have moved from a wet, almost subtropical region with many streams to the margins of the Great Plains. In doing so they have restructured their economy many times and have undergone radical changes in their politics and religion. So why would we think that modern Creeks can help us understand their Lamar ancestors of five hundred years ago?

In the case of the conch shells, we find an amazing continuity in their respect for this object, even though it was probably redefined in function from conch dipper to conch trumpet. The spiral design of the shell remains an important symbol as well. For example, in 1984 stomp grounds and churches were invited to submit letterhead designs to receive free stationery from the Tribal Towns Center. Many submitted designs with spirals, but under different rationales. To some the spiral represented the line of buffalo dancers around the ball pole, to others it was the wandering and suffering of the Mvskoke people, and to others it represented the search for Jesus.

There are also implicit meanings to be deciphered from the spiral. It seems clear, for example, that at the stomp grounds dancers usually dance in a spiral around the ball pole when men and women are both in the line. Exclusively male or female groups dance in a circle rather than a spiral. Symbolically, the circle might thus imply sexual separatism and the spiral a mixing of the sexes.

In any event, such symbols as the spiral, the medicine kettle, the ball stick, and the ceremonial fire/Christian cross are best interpreted as what Victor Turner calls multivocal symbols (Turner 1970). And if the explanations offered by modern Creeks for these symbols and ritual objects are not always consistent or historically accurate, they at least help to set a narrower range of possibilities for archaeological interpretation. For example, no Creek would think to "listen to the sea" in a conch shell or maintain that it had anything at all to do with symbolizing marine life. Nor is it interpreted as a symbol of war, as it was in Meso-America. Recent Creek ethnography indicates that the conch has something to do with ceremonial life, and that the spiral is the key symbolic element, whatever its interpretation.

Concerning burials, the examples from Creek ethnography can go much further in elucidating archaeological evidence than one might imagine, but an important lesson here is that modern tribal peoples are often circumspect in explaining themselves and their traditions to outsiders. When white people visit a Mvskoke Baptist church, for example, the members emphasize their similarities with other Baptists and other Christians. One would not learn initially that the pastor is also a medicine man, or that pastors frequently accuse one another of witchcraft, using the traditional idiom. And I doubt that any woman entering a local non-Indian Baptist church would be asked if she were menstruating and seated accordingly.

I began this essay with a plea for cooperation between ethnologists and archaeologists to use ethnographic analogy for the maximum benefit to both fields. For this kind of collaboration to proceed effectively, archaeologists must recognize that ethnographic inquiries useful for analogy cannot be accomplished quickly and must be undertaken by someone with ethnographic skills. One cannot simply drop by a medicine man's house and ask him how burials are oriented. A long, trusting relationship is necessary, and even then an ethnographer cannot ask just anything. Frequently, he or she must just hang around and wait for certain topics to come up in conversation, if they ever do.

But conversely, ethnologists need to understand archaeologists' problems and be educated to the fact that some of their results might be useful to archaeologists. Recent specializations in our discipline, unfortunately, have created ethnologists and social and cultural anthropologists with little training in archaeology and consequently little appreciation for the class of problems archaeologists confront. In general, to collaborate effectively with archaeologists, ethnologists must pay more attention to material culture and to the behavior that creates it. Ethnologists must read the archaeological literature so that we know what problems are currently significant.

I hope that archaeologists can reciprocate and help develop a common vocabulary with ethnologists for considering matters of kinship and political organization. In the Southeast, for example, the archaeological consideration of chiefships seems to be drifting away from the ethnological mainstream, both in theory and in vocabulary, and this can only create problems in the future. Ethnologists must criticize archaeological writing, and archaeologists must challenge the ideas of ethnologists. I hope that this essay is a step in that direction, and I welcome critical comments.

NOTE

For their consultations and assistance I especially thank Toney E. Hill, Mekko Tastake of the Mvskokullke Etvlwa Etelaketa; Otis B. Harjo; Linda Alexander; Bertha Tilkens; Pastor Joe Smith; Joe Cook; the late José Hicks; the late Pastor Martin Givens; and the late George Cosar, Sr. For their collegial assistance I thank Jerald Milanich, James Hatch, Aaron Broadwell, and Jack Schultz.

References

Abbott, R. Tucker. 1962. *Sea Shells of the World.* New York: Golden Press.

Adair, James, and Samuel Williams. 1974. *Adair's History of the American Indians.* New York: Promontory Press.

Anderson, David G. 1987. Warfare and Mississippian Political Evolution in the Southeastern United States. Paper presented at the Twentieth Annual Chacmool Conference, Calgary.

————. 1990. *Political Change in Chiefdom Societies: Cycling in the Late Prehistoric Southeastern United States.* Ph.D. dissertation, University of Michigan. Ann Arbor: University Microfilms.

————. 1992. Factional Competition and the Political Evolution of Mississippian Chiefdoms in the Southeastern United States. Unpublished manuscript in author's files.

Argüelles, Antonio de. 1677. Visitation of Guale and Mocama, 1677. Trans. John H. Hann. In Visitations and Revolts in Florida, 1656–1695. *Florida Archaeology* 7:83–94.

Atkinson, James R. 1975. Rolling Hills: A Late Mississippian/Early Historic Site in the Tombigbee River Drainage of Northeast Mississippi. Typescript on file at the Cobb Institute of Archaeology, Mississippi State University, Starkville.

————. 1976. Cultural Resources Reconnaissance, Edinburg Lake, Pearl River Basin, Mississippi. Report submitted to the U.S. Army Corps of Engineers. Department of Anthropology, Mississippi State University, Starkville.

————. 1979. A Historic Contact Indian Settlement in Oktibbeha County, Mississippi. *Journal of Alabama Archaeology* 25:61–82.

————. 1987. The de Soto Expedition Through North Mississippi in 1540–41. *Mississippi Archaeology* 22:61–73.

Atkinson, James R., and Crawford H. Blakeman. 1975. Archaeological Site Survey in the Tallahala Reservoir Area, Jasper County, Mississippi: 1975. Report submitted to the Department of the Interior, National Park Service. Department of Anthropology, Mississippi State University, Starkville.

Ballard, W. L. 1973. English-Yuchi Lexicon. Unpublished manuscript in author's files.

————. 1982. Lexical Borrowing Among Southeastern Native American Languages. In *1982 Mid-America Linguistics Conference Papers,* ed. Frances

Ingemann, pp. 325–34. Lawrence: Department of Linguistics, University of Kansas.

Bauxar, J. Joseph. 1957. Yuchi Ethnoarchaeology. *Ethnohistory* 4:279–301, 369–464.

Berquin-Duvallon. 1803. *Vue de la colonie espagnole du Mississipi, ou des provinces de Louisiane et Floride Occidentale, en l'année 1802, par un observateur résident sur les lieux.* Paris: Imprimerie expéditive.

Best, Elsdon. 1925. *The Maori Canoe.* Dominion Museum Bulletin no. 7. Wellington, New Zealand.

Binford, Lewis R. 1978. *Nunamiut Ethnoarchaeology.* New York: Academic Press.

———. 1992. Ethnoarchaeology of Hunters and Gatherers. Lecture to Department of Anthropology, University of Oklahoma, February 2.

Binford, Sally R., and Lewis R. Binford. 1968. *New Perspectives in Archeology.* Chicago: Aldine.

Bizzell, David W. 1981. A Report on the Quapaw: The Letters of Governor George Izard to the American Philosophical Society, 1825–1827. *Pulaski County Historical Review* 29:66–79.

Blitz, John H. 1985. An Archaeological Study of the Mississippi Choctaw Indians. Mississippi Department of Archives and History Archaeological Reports, no. 16.

Bloomfield, Leonard. 1946. Algonquian. In *Linguistic Structures of Native America,* ed. Harry Hoijer, pp. 85–129. Viking Fund Publications in Anthropology, no. 6. New York.

Boas, Franz. 1906. Notes on the Ponca Grammar. *15th International Congress of Americanists* 2:317–37.

Boas, Franz, and Ella Deloria. 1939. *Dakota Grammar.* Memoirs of the National Academy of Sciences 23.

Booker, Maren M. 1980. Comparative Muskogean: Aspects of Proto-Muskogean Verb Morphology. Ph.D. dissertation, University of Kansas.

Boudinot, Elias. 1832. Invention of a New Alphabet. *American Annals of Education* (April).

Brain, Jeffrey P. 1979. *The Tunica Treasure.* Papers of the Peabody Museum of Archaeology and Ethnology 71. Cambridge: Harvard University Press.

———. 1984. The de Soto Entrada into the Lower Mississippi Valley. *Mississippi Archaeology* 19:48–58.

———. 1985a. The Archaeology of the Hernando de Soto Expedition. In *Alabama and the Borderlands: From Prehistory to Statehood,* ed. Reid Badger and Lawrence A. Clayton, pp. 96–107. University: University of Alabama Press.

———. 1985b. Introduction: Update of de Soto Studies Since the United

States de Soto Commission Report. In *Final Report of the U.S. de Soto Expedition Commission*, pp. xi–lvi. Washington, D.C.: Smithsonian Institution Press.

———. 1988. *Tunica Archaeology*. Peabody Museum of Archaeology and Ethnology. Cambridge: Harvard University Press.

———. 1990. *The Tunica-Biloxi*. New York: Chelsea House.

Brain, Jeffrey P., Alan Toth, and Antonio Rodriquez-Buckingham. 1974. Ethnohistoric Archaeology and the de Soto Entrada into the Lower Mississippi Valley. *Conference on Historic Site Archaeology Papers* 8:232–89.

Broadwell, George A. 1993. Subtractive Morphology in Southwest Muskogean. *International Journal of American Linguistics* 59.

Brown, Ian W. 1985. Natchez Indian Archaeology: Culture Change and Stability in the Lower Mississippi Valley. Mississippi Department of Archives and History Archaeological Reports, no. 15.

Brown, James. 1985. The Mississippian Period. In *Ancient Art of the American Woodland Indians*, ed. David Brose, James Brown, and David Penny, pp. 93–145. New York: Harry Abrams.

Brown, James A., Richard A. Kerber, and Howard D. Winters. 1990. Trade and the Evolution of Exchange Relations at the Beginning of the Mississippian Period. In *The Mississippian Emergence*, ed. Bruce D. Smith, pp. 251–80. Washington, D.C.: Smithsonian Institution Press.

Bushnell, G. H. S. 1965. *Ancient Art of the Americas*. New York: Praeger.

Byington, Cyrus. 1915. *A Dictionary of the Choctaw Language*. Ed. John R. Swanton and Henry Halbert. Bureau of American Ethnology Bulletin 46. Washington, D.C.

Campbell, Lyle, Terrence Kaufman, and Thomas C. Smith-Stark. 1986. Meso-America as a Linguistic Area. *Language* 62:530–70.

Carleton, Kenneth H. 1992. Choctaw Ceramic Typology: An Overview and Additions Based on Recent Work in the Choctaw Homeland. Paper presented at the Thirteenth Annual Midsouth Archaeological Conference, Moundville State Monument, May 23–24, 1992.

Carneiro, Robert L. 1970. A Theory of the Origin of the State. *Science* 169:733–38.

———. 1981. The Chiefdom: Precursor of the State. In *The Transition to Statehood in the New World*, ed. Grant D. Jones and Robert R. Kautz, pp. 37–79. New York: Cambridge University Press.

———. 1990. Chiefdom-Level Warfare as Exemplified in Fiji and the Cauca Valley. In *The Anthropology of War*, ed. Jonathan Haas, pp. 190–211. Cambridge: Cambridge University Press.

Chafe, Wallace L. 1967. *Seneca Morphology and Dictionary*. Washington, D.C.: Smithsonian Institution Press.

————. 1970. *A Semantically Based Sketch of Onondaga.* Indiana University Publications in Anthropology and Linguistics, Memoir 25.

————. 1976. *The Caddoan, Iroquoian, and Siouan Languages.* The Hague: Mouton.

Chapman, Carl H. 1980. *The Archaeology of Missouri.* Vol. 2. Columbia: University of Missouri Press.

Chardon, Roland. 1980. The Elusive Spanish League: A Problem of Measurement in Sixteenth-Century New Spain. *Hispanic American Historical Review* 60:294–302.

Cherokee Phoenix. 1828–34. New Echota: Cherokee Nation.

Chiefs of Apalachee. 1688. Letter to the King, San Luis de Abalachi, 21st day of the Moon that is called January. Trans. from the Apalachee by Fray Marcelo de San Joseph. Archivo General de las Indias, Santo Domingo 839, Stetson Collection.

Collins, Henry B., Jr. 1927. Potsherds from Choctaw Village Sites in Mississippi. *Journal of the Washington Academy of Sciences* 17:259–63.

Conn, Thomas L. 1978. Archaeological Investigations at 22Ld515, Lauderdale County Northeast Industrial Park, Lauderdale County, Mississippi. Report submitted to Lauderdale County. Department of Anthropology, Mississippi State University, Starkville.

Crawford, James M. 1975. Southeastern Indian Languages. In *Studies in Southeastern Indian Languages*, ed. James M. Crawford, pp. 1–120. Athens: University of Georgia Press.

————. 1978. *The Mobilian Trade Language.* Knoxville: University of Tennessee Press.

D'Anville. 1752. *Carte de la Louisiane.* Map in the Louisiana Collection, Tulane University.

DePratter, Chester B. 1983. *Late Prehistoric and Early Historic Chiefdoms in the Southeastern United States.* Ph.D. dissertation, University of Georgia. Ann Arbor: University Microfilms.

Dickinson, Samuel D. 1980. Historic Tribes of the Ouachita Drainage System in Arkansas. *Arkansas Archeologist* 21:1–11.

Dickson, D. Bruce. 1981. The Yanomamö of the Mississippi Valley? Some Reflections on Larson (1972), Gibson (1974), and Mississippian Period Warfare in the Southeastern United States. *American Antiquity* 46:909–16.

Dorsey, James Owen, and John R. Swanton. 1912. *A Dictionary of the Biloxi and Ofo Languages, Accompanied with Thirty-one Biloxi Texts and Numerous Biloxi Phrases.* Bureau of American Ethnology Bulletin 47. Washington, D.C.

Drechsel, Emanuel J. 1981. A Preliminary Sociolinguistic Comparison of Four Indigenous Pidgin Languages of North America (with Notes Towards a

Sociolinguistic Typology in American Indian Linguistics). *Anthropological Linguistics* 23:93–112.

———. 1983. The Question of the Lingua Franca Creek. In *1982 Mid-America Linguistics Conference Papers*, ed. Frances Ingemann, pp. 388–400. Lawrence: Department of Linguistics, University of Kansas.

———. 1984. Structure and Function in Mobilian Jargon: Indications for the Pre-European Existence of an American Indian Pidgin. *Journal of Historical Linguistics and Philology* 1:141–85.

———. 1987. Meta-Communicative Functions of Mobilian Jargon, an American Indian Pidgin of the Lower Mississippi River Region. In *Pidgin and Creole Languages. Essays in Memory of John E. Reinecke*, ed. Glenn G. Gilbert, pp. 433–44. Honolulu: University Press of Hawaii.

———. In press. *Mobilian Jargon: Linguistic and Sociohistorical Aspects of an American Pidgin*. Oxford: Oxford University Press.

Dumont de Montigny, Jean Benjamin François. 1747. Memoire De Lxx Dxx Officier Ingenieur, Contenant les Evenemens qui se sont passés à la Louisiane depuis 1715 jusqu'à présent ainsi que ses remarques sur les moeurs, usages et forces des diverses nations de l'Amerique Septentrionale et de ses productions. Manuscript, Ayer Collection, Newberry Library, Chicago.

———. 1753. *Mémoires historiques sur la Louisiane, contenant ce qui y est arrivé de plus mémorable depuis l'année 1687, jusqu'à présent*. 2 vols. Paris: C. J. B. Bauche.

Dye, David H. 1990. Warfare in the Sixteenth-Century Southeast: The de Soto Expedition in the Interior. In *Columbian Consequences*, vol. 2, ed. David H. Thomas, pp. 211–22. Washington, D.C.: Smithsonian Institution Press.

———. 1992. The Hernando de Soto Expedition in the Mississippi Alluvial Plain. Unpublished manuscript in author's files.

Dye, David H., and Cheryl Anne Cox, eds. 1990. *Towns and Temples Along the Mississippi*. Tuscaloosa: University of Alabama Press.

Earle, Timothy K. 1989. The Evolution of Chiefdoms. *Current Anthropology* 30:84–88.

Elvas, A Fidalgo of. 1922. True Relation of the Vicissitudes that Attended the Governor Don Hernando de Soto and Some Nobles of Portugal in the Discovery of the Province of Florida. In *Narratives of the Career of Hernando de Soto in the Conquest of Florida*, ed. Edward G. Bourne, trans. Buckingham Smith, vol. 1:1–223. New York: A. S. Barnes.

Emerson, Thomas E., and R. Barry Lewis, eds. 1991. *Cahokia and the Hinterlands: Middle Mississippian Cultures of the Midwest*. Urbana: University of Illinois Press.

Fairbanks, Charles. 1952. Creek and Pre-Creek. In *Archeology of Eastern*

United States, ed. James B. Griffin, pp. 285–300. Chicago: University of Chicago Press.

Ferguson, R. Brian, and Neil L. Whitehead. 1992. The Violent Edge of Empire. In *War in the Tribal Zone: Expanding States and Indigenous Warfare*, ed. R. Brian Ferguson and Neil L. Whitehead, pp. 1–30. Santa Fe: School of American Research Press.

Fernández de Ecija, Francisco. 1605. Translation of the Ecija Voyages of 1605 and 1609 and the González Derrotero of 1609. Trans. John N. Hann. *Florida Archaeology* 2:1–80.

Fernández de Florencia, Juan. 1675. Autos Concerning the Tumult of the Chacatos. Trans. John H. Hann. In Visitations and Revolts. *Florida Archaeology* 7:147–51.

Fernández de Oviedo y Valdés, Gonzalo. 1851. *Historia General y Natural de las Indias, Islas Y Tierra-Firme del Mar Oceano*. 4 vols. Madrid: Imprenta de la Real Academia de la Historia.

Florencia, Joachin de. 1695. Visitation of Apalachee and Timuqua. Trans. John H. Hann. In Visitations and Revolts. *Florida Archaeology* 7:152–95.

Fogelson, Raymond D. 1974. On the Varieties of Indian History. *Journal of Ethnic History* 2:105–12.

―――. 1980. The Conjuror in Eastern Cherokee Society. *Journal of Cherokee Studies* 5:60–87.

Ford, James A. 1936. Analysis of Indian Village Site Collections from Louisiana and Mississippi. Louisiana Department of Conservation, Anthropological Study no. 2. Louisiana Geological Survey, New Orleans.

―――. 1961. *Menard Site: The Quapaw Village of Osotouy on the Arkansas River*. Anthropological Papers of the American Museum of Natural History no. 49, pt. 2. New York.

Foreman, Grant, ed. 1930. *A Traveler in Indian Territory: The Journal of Ethan Allen Hitchcock, Late Major-General of the United States Army*. Cedar Rapids, Iowa: Torch Press.

―――. 1938. *Sequoyah*. Norman: University of Oklahoma Press.

Fuller, Richard S. 1992. Protohistoric and Early Historic Period Phases and Complexes in the Forks Region. Manuscript on file, University of Alabama Museum of Natural History, Tuscaloosa.

Fuller, Richard S., Diane E. Silvia, and Noel R. Stowe. 1984. The Forks Project: An Investigation of the Late Prehistoric–Early Historic Transition in the Alabama-Tombigbee Confluence Basin, Phase 1: Preliminary Survey. Report Submitted to the Alabama Historical Commission. University of South Alabama Archaeological Research Laboratory, Mobile.

Galloway, Patricia K. 1982. Sources for the La Salle Expedition of 1682. In *La Salle and His Legacy: Frenchmen and Indians in the Lower Mississippi Valley*, pp. 11–40. Jackson: University Press of Mississippi.

————. 1984. Technical Origins for Chickachae Combed Ceramics: An Ethnohistorical Hypothesis. *Mississippi Archaeology* 19:58–66.

————, ed. 1989. *The Southeastern Ceremonial Complex: Artifacts and Analysis.* Lincoln: University of Nebraska Press.

————. 1991. The Archaeology of Ethnohistorical Narrative. In *Columbian Consequences,* vol. 3, ed. David H. Thomas, pp. 453–69. Washington, D.C.: Smithsonian Institution Press.

————. 1994. Confederacy as a Solution to Chiefdom Dissolution: Historical Evidence in the Choctaw Case. In *The Forgotten Centuries, Indians and Europeans in the American South, 1521–1704,* ed. Charles M. Hudson and Carmen Tesser. Athens: University of Georgia Press.

Gatschet, Albert S. 1878. The Timucua Language. Paper read before the American Philosophical Society, April 5th, 1878. *Proceedings of the American Philosophical Society* 16:490–504.

————. 1884 [1969]. *A Migration Legend of the Creek Indians, with a Linguistic, Historic and Ethnographic Introduction.* Vol. 1. Philadelphia: D. G. Brinton. Reprint. New York: Kraus Reprint Company.

————. 1892. Tchikilli's Kash'hta Legend in the Creek and Hitchiti Languages, with a Critical Commentary and Full Glossaries of Both Texts. *Transactions of the Academy of Sciences of St. Louis* 5:33–239.

Gatschet, Albert S., and John R. Swanton. 1932. *A Dictionary of the Atakapa Language (Accompanied by Text Material).* Bureau of American Ethnology Bulletin 108. Washington, D.C.

Gibson, Jon L. 1974. Aboriginal Warfare in the Protohistoric Southeast: An Alternative Perspective. *American Antiquity* 39:130–33.

Gilman, Patricia A. 1987. Architecture as Artifact: Pit Structures and Pueblos in the American Southwest. *American Antiquity* 52:538–64.

Glassow, Michael A. 1972. Changes in the Adaptations of Southwestern Basketmakers: A Systems Perspective. In *Contemporary Archaeology,* ed. Mark P. Leone, pp. 289–302. Carbondale: Southern Illinois Press.

Gould, Richard A. 1980. *Living Archaeology.* New York: Cambridge University Press.

Granberry, Julian. 1987. *A Grammar and Dictionary of the Timucua Language.* 2d ed. Horseshoe Beach, Fla.: Island Archaeological Museum.

————. 1990. A Grammatical Sketch of Timucua. *International Journal of American Linguistics* 56:60–101.

Griffin, James B. 1990. Comments on the Late Prehistoric Societies in the Southeast. In *Towns and Temples Along the Mississippi,* ed. David H. Dye and Cheryl A. Cox, pp. 5–15. Tuscaloosa: University of Alabama Press.

Haag, William G. 1953. Choctaw Archaeology. *Southeastern Archaeological Conference Newsletter* 3:25–28.

Haas, Mary R. c. 1940. Creek Vocabulary. Unpublished manuscript.

——— . 1941 [1960]. The Classification of the Muskogean Languages. In *Language, Culture, and Personality: Essays in Memory of Edward Sapir*, ed. L. Spier et al., pp. 41–56. Menasha, Wisc.: Banta Publishing. Reprint, Salt Lake City: University of Utah Press.

——— . 1945. Dialects of the Muskogee Language. *International Journal of American Linguistics* 11:69–74.

——— . 1946a. A Grammatical Sketch of Tunica. In *Linguistic Structures of Native America*, ed. Harry Hoijer, pp. 337–66. New York: Viking Fund.

——— . 1946b. A Proto-Muskogean Paradigm. *Language* 22:326–32.

——— . 1947. Development of Proto-Muskogean *k*ʷ. *International Journal of American Linguistics* 13:135–37.

——— . 1950. *Tunica Texts*. University of California Publications in Linguistics 6. Berkeley: University of California Press.

——— . 1951. The Proto-Gulf Word for *Water* (with Notes on Siouan-Yuchi). *International Journal of American Linguistics* 17:71–79.

——— . 1952. The Proto-Gulf Word for *Land*. *International Journal of American Linguistics* 18:238–40.

——— . 1953. *Tunica Dictionary*. University of California Publications in Linguistics 6, pt. 2. Berkeley: University of California Press.

——— . 1956. Natchez and the Muskogean Languages. *Language* 32:61–72.

——— . 1958. A New Linguistic Relationship in North America: Algonkian and the Gulf Languages. *Southwestern Journal of Anthropology* 14:231–64.

——— . 1961. Comment on Floyd G. Lounsbury's "Iroquois-Cherokee Linguistic Relations." In *Symposium on Cherokee and Iroquois Culture*, ed. W. Fenton and J. Gulick. Bureau of American Ethnology Bulletin 180, pp. 19–23. Washington, D.C.

——— . 1968. The Last Words of Biloxi. *International Journal of American Linguistics* 34:77–88.

——— . 1969. *The Prehistory of Languages*. The Hague: Mouton.

——— . 1971. Southeastern Indian Linguistics. In *Red, White, and Black*, ed. Charles M. Hudson, pp. 44–54. Southern Anthropological Society Proceedings, no. 5. Athens: University of Georgia Press.

——— . 1973. The Southeast. In *Current Trends in Linguistics*, ed. Thomas A. Sebeok. Vol. 10: *Linguistics in North America*, pp. 1210–49. The Hague: Mouton.

——— . 1977. Anthropological Linguistics: History. In *Perspectives on Anthropology 1976*, ed. Anthony F. C. Wallace, J. Lawrence Angel, Richard Fox, Sally McLendon, Rachael Sady, and Robert Sharer, pp. 33–47. Special Publication of the American Anthropological Association no. 10. Washington, D.C.: American Anthropological Association.

——— . 1979a. The Auxiliary Verb in Natchez. In *Proceedings of the Fifth*

Annual Meeting of the Berkeley Linguistics Society, ed. Christine Chiarello et al., pp. 94–105. Berkeley: Berkeley Linguistics Society.

————. 1979b. Southeastern Languages. In *The Languages of Native North America: Historical and Comparative Assessment*, ed. Lyle Campbell and Marianne Mithun, pp. 299–326. Austin: University of Texas Press.

Halbert, Henry S. 1901. District Divisions of the Choctaw Nation. Publications of the Alabama Historical Society, Miscellaneous Collection, 1:375–85.

Hann, John H. 1988. *Apalachee: The Land Between the Rivers*. Gainesville: University of Florida Press and Florida State Museum.

————. 1991. *Missions to the Calusa*. Gainesville: University of Florida Press and Florida Museum of Natural History.

————. 1992. Heathen Acuera, Murder, and a Potano Cimarrona: The St. Johns River and the Alachua Prairie in the 1670s. *Florida Historical Quarterly* 70:451–74.

Hatch, James W. 1975. Social Dimensions of Dallas Burials. *Southeastern Archaeological Conference Bulletin* 18:132–38.

Hawkins, Benjamin. 1982. *Letters of Benjamin Hawkins, 1796–1806*. Originally published in 1848 as vol. 3, pt. 1, of Collections of the Georgia Historical Society. Reprint. Spartanburg, S.C.: The Reprint Company.

Helms, Mary W. 1979. *Ancient Panama: Chiefs in Search of Power*. Austin: University of Texas Press.

Henige, David. 1986. The Context, Content, and Credibility of *La Florida del Ynca*. *The Americas* 43:1–23.

Hernández de Biedma, Luys. 1857. Relación Verdadera. In *Colección de Varios Documentos para la Historia de la Florida y Tierras Adjacentes*, ed. Buckingham Smith. London: Casa Trubner.

————. 1922. Relation of the Conquest of Florida Presented by Luys Hernandez de Biedma in the Year 1544 to the King of Spain in Council. In *Narratives of the Career of Hernando de Soto in the Conquest of Florida*, ed. Edward G. Bourne, trans. Buckingham Smith, 2:3–40. New York: A. S. Barnes.

Hitchcock, Ethan Allen. 1930. *A Traveler in Indian Territory*. Ed. Grant Foreman. Cedar Rapids, Iowa: Torch Press.

Hoffman, Michael P. 1977. The Kinkead-Mainard Site, 3PU2: A Late Prehistoric Quapaw Phase Site near Little Rock, Arkansas. *Arkansas Archeologist* 16–18:1–41.

————. 1986. The Protohistoric Period in the Lower and Central River Valley in Arkansas. In *The Protohistoric Period in the Mid-South: 1500–1700*, ed. David H. Dye and Ronald C. Brister, pp. 24–37. Mississippi Department of Archives and History Archaeological Reports, no. 18.

————. 1990. The Terminal Mississippian Period in the Arkansas River Valley and Quapaw Ethnogenesis. In *Towns and Temples Along the Mississippi*, ed. David H. Dye and Cheryl A. Cox, pp. 208–26. Tuscaloosa: University of Alabama Press.

———. 1992. Protohistoric Period Tunican Indians in Arkansas. *Arkansas Historical Quarterly* 51:30–53.

Holland, Thomas D. 1991. An Archaeological and Biological Analysis of the Campbell Site. Ph.D. dissertation, University of Missouri.

House, John H. 1987. Kent Phase Investigations in Eastern Arkansas, 1978–1984. *Mississippi Archeology* 22:46–60.

Howard, James H. 1968. *The Southeastern Ceremonial Complex and Its Interpretation*. Missouri Archaeological Society Memoir, no. 6.

Hudson, Charles. 1976. *The Southeastern Indians*. Knoxville: University of Tennessee Press.

———. 1985. *De Soto in Arkansas: A Brief Synopsis*. Arkansas Archeological Survey, Field Notes 205:3–12.

———. 1987. Juan Pardo's Excursion Beyond Chiaha. *Tennessee Anthropologist* 12:74–87.

———. 1990. *The Juan Pardo Expeditions: Explorations of the Carolinas and Tennessee, 1566–1568*. Washington, D.C.: Smithsonian Institution Press.

Hudson, Charles, Chester B. DePratter, and Marvin T. Smith. 1989. Hernando de Soto's Expedition Through the Southern United States. In *First Encounters: Spanish Explorations in the Caribbean and the United States, 1492–1570*, ed. Jerald T. Milanich and Susan Milbrath, pp. 77–98. Gainesville: University Presses of Florida.

Hudson, Charles, Marvin T. Smith, and Chester B. DePratter. 1984. The Hernando de Soto Expedition: From Apalachee to Chiaha. *Southeastern Archaeology* 3:65–77.

Hudson, Charles, Marvin T. Smith, and Chester B. DePratter. 1990. The Hernando de Soto Expedition: From Mabila to the Mississippi River. In *Towns and Temples Along the Mississippi*, ed. David H. Dye and Cheryl A. Cox, pp. 175–201. Tuscaloosa: University of Alabama Press.

Ibarra, Pedro de. 1604 [1912]. Relación del viaje que hizó el señor Pedro de Ibarra, Gobernador y Capitán General de la Florida, á visitar los pueblos de Indios de las Provincias de San Pedro y Guale. In *Documentos Históricos de la Florida y la Luisiana, siglos XVI al XVIII*, ed. Manuel Serrano y Sanz. Madrid: Libreria General de Victoriano Suárez.

Indian Affairs. Census of 1835 (M-496). Record Group 75. National Archives. Washington, D.C.

Jacob, Betty, Dale Nicklas, and Betty Lou Spencer. 1977. *Introduction to Choctaw*. Durant, Okla.: Choctaw Bilingual Education Program, Southeastern Oklahoma State University.

Jeter, Marvin. 1986. Tunicans West of the Mississippi: A Summary of Early Historic and Archeological Evidence. In *The Protohistoric Period in the Mid-South, 1500–1700,* ed. David H. Dye and Ronald C. Brister, pp. 324–37. Mississippi Department of History and Archives Archaeological Reports, no. 18.

Jeter, Marvin, K. H. Cande, and J. J. Mintz, eds. 1989. Goldsmith Oliver 2 (3PU306): A Protohistoric Archeological Site near Little Rock, Arkansas. Draft report submitted by the Arkansas Archeological Survey to the Federal Aviation Administration, Southwest Region.

Johnson, Allen W., and Timothy Earle. 1987. *The Evolution of Human Societies: From Foraging Group to Agrarian State.* Stanford: Stanford University Press.

Kerr, Justin. 1990. *The Maya Vase Book.* Vol. 2. New York: Kerr Associates.

Kilpatrick, Jack Frederick, and Anna Gritts Kilpatrick. 1965. *The Shadow of Sequoyah: Social Documents of the Cherokees, 1862–1964.* Norman: University of Oklahoma Press.

Kimball, Geoffrey. 1985. A Descriptive Grammar of Koasati. Ph.D. dissertation, Tulane University.

———. 1987. A Grammatical Sketch of Apalachee. *International Journal of American Linguistics* 53:136–74.

———. 1988. An Apalachee Vocabulary. *International Journal of American Linguistics* 54:387–98.

———. 1990. The Proto-Muskogean Numeral System. In *1990 Mid-America Linguistics Conference Papers,* ed. Frances Ingemann, pp. 197–213. Lawrence: Department of Linguistics, University of Kansas.

———. 1991. *Koasati Grammar.* Lincoln: University of Nebraska Press.

Knight, Vernon James, Jr. 1986. The Institutional Organization of Mississippian Religion. *American Antiquity* 51:675–87.

———. 1990. Social Organization and the Evolution of Hierarchy in Southeastern Chiefdoms. *Journal of Anthropological Research* 46:1–23.

Lafferty, Robert H., III. 1973. An Analysis of Prehistoric Southeastern Fortifications. Master's thesis, Southern Illinois University at Carbondale.

———. 1977. The Evolution of the Mississippian Settlement Pattern and Exploitative Technology in the Black Bottom of Southern Illinois. Ph.D. dissertation, Southern Illinois University at Carbondale.

———. 1986. A Review of Ethnohistoric and Archaeological Evidence of Riverine Canoe Facilities of the Eastern United States. Paper presented at the Fifty-first Annual Meeting of the Society for American Archaeology, New Orleans.

Lankford, George E. 1992. "Reysed After There Manner." *Arkansas Archeologist* 31:65–71.

Lanning, John Tate. 1935. *The Spanish Missions of Georgia*. Chapel Hill: University of North Carolina Press.

Larson, Lewis H. 1972. Functional Considerations of Warfare in the Southeast During the Mississippian Period. *American Antiquity* 37:383–92.

———. 1978. Historic Guale Indians of the Georgia Coast and the Impact of the Spanish Mission Effort. In *Tacachale: Essays on the Indians of Florida and Southeastern Georgia During the Historic Period*, ed. Jerald T. Milanich and Samuel Proctor, pp. 120–40. Ripley P. Bullen Monographs in Anthropology and History, no. 1. Gainesville: University Presses of Florida.

Le Page du Pratz, Antoine Simon. 1758. *Histoire de la Louisiane, contenant la découverte de ce vaste pays; sa description géographique; un voyage dans les terres; l'histoire naturelle; les moeurs, coûtumes & religion des naturels, avec leurs origines; deux voyages dans le nord du nouveau Mexique, dont un jus-qu'à la mer de Sud*. 3 vols. Paris: De Bure.

Leturiondo, Domingo de. 1677. Visitation of the Province of Apalachee and Timuqua. Trans. John H. Hann. In Visitations and Revolts. *Florida Archaeology* 7:95–146.

Lewis, Theodore H. 1902. Route of de Soto's Expedition from Taliepacana to Huhasene. *Mississippi Historical Society Publication* 6:449–67.

Lewis, Thomas M. N., and Madeline Kneberg. 1946. *Hiwassee Island*. Knoxville: University of Tennessee Press.

Lorant, Stefan, ed. 1965. *The First Pictures of America Made by John White and Jacques Le Moyne and Engraved by Theodore de Bry with Contemporary Narratives of the French Settlements in Florida, 1562–1565 and the English Colonies in Virginia, 1585–1590*. Rev. ed. New York: Duell, Sloan and Pearse.

Lounsbury, Floyd G. 1961. Iroquois-Cherokee Linguistic Relations. In *Symposium on Cherokee and Iroquois Culture*, ed. W. Fenton and J. Gulick, pp. 9–17. Bureau of American Ethnology Bulletin 180. Washington, D.C.

Lupardus, Karen J. 1982. The Language of the Alabama Indians. Ph.D. dissertation, University of Kansas.

Lussagnet, Suzanne, ed. 1958. *Les Français en Amérique Pendant la Deuxième Moitié de XVIe Siècle. Les Français en Floride, Textes de Jean Ribault, René de Laudonnière, Nicolas le Challeux et Dominique de Gourges*. Paris: Presses Universitaires de France.

McLoughlin, William G. 1984a. *The Cherokee Ghost Dance: Essays on the Southeastern Indians, 1789–1861*. Macon, Ga.: Mercer University Press.

———. 1984b. *Cherokees and Missionaries, 1789–1839*. New Haven: Yale University Press.

———. 1986. *Cherokee Renascence in the New Republic*. Princeton: Princeton University Press.

McWilliams, Richebourg G., trans. and ed. 1981. *Iberville's Gulf Journals.* Tuscaloosa: University of Alabama Press.

Malone, Henry T. 1956. *Cherokees of the Old South: A People in Transition.* Athens: University of Georgia Press.

Mann, Cyril B., Jr. 1983. Classification of Ceramics from the Lubbub Creek Archaeological Locality. In Prehistoric Agricultural Communities in West Central Alabama, Studies of Material Remains from the Lubbub Creek Archaeological Locality, ed. Christopher S. Peebles, 2:2–121. Report submitted to the U.S. Army Corps of Engineers. University of Michigan, Ann Arbor.

————. 1988. Archaeological Classification of Ceramics from the Pearl River Mounds (22Lw510) Lawrence County, Mississippi. Master's thesis, University of Southern Mississippi.

Marshall, Richard A. 1992. The Starkville Complex and the Chakchiuma. Paper presented at the Thirteenth Annual Midsouth Archaeological Conference, Moundville State Monument, May 23–24, 1992.

Martin, Paul S., and Fred Plog. 1973. *The Archaeology of Arizona.* Garden City, N.Y.: Natural History Press for the American Museum of Natural History.

Matheos, Antonio. 1686. Letter to Governor Juan Marques Cabrera, San Luis, May 31, 1686, in Viceroy of Mexico, Count of Paredes and Marquis of Laguna, letter to the King, July 19, 1686. Archivo General de las Indias, Mexico, 56, John Tate Lanning Collection of the Thomas Jefferson Library of the University of Missouri, St. Louis, vol. 5 of Colección "Misiones Guale."

————. 1688. Testimony from the record of the residencia of Juan Marques Cabrera. Archivo General de las Indias, Escribánia de Cámara, leg. 156C, pieza 25, E. 20, Santo Domingo, Stetson Collection.

Michelson, Truman. 1935. Phonetic Shifts in Algonquian Languages. *International Journal of American Linguistics* 8:131–71.

Milanich, Jerald T. 1978. The Western Timucua: Patterns of Acculturation and Change. In *Tacachale: Essays on the Indians of Florida and Southeastern Georgia During the Historic Period,* ed. Jerald T. Milanich and Samuel Proctor, pp. 59–88. Gainesville: University Presses of Florida.

————. 1979. Origins and Prehistoric Distributions of Black Drink and the Ceremonial Shell Drinking Cup. In *Black Drink,* ed. Charles H. Hudson, pp. 83–119. Athens: University of Georgia Press.

Milanich, Jerald T., and William C. Sturtevant. 1972. *Francisco Pareja's 1613 Confessionario.* Tallahassee: Division of Archives, History, and Records Management, Florida Department of State.

Miller, Wick R. 1959. An Outline of Shawnee Historical Phonology. *International Journal of American Linguistics* 25:16–21.

Milner, George R., Eve Anderson, and Virginia G. Smith. 1991. Warfare in Late Prehistoric West-Central Illinois. *American Antiquity* 56:581–603.

Minnis, Paul E. 1985. *Social Adaptation to Food Stress*. Chicago: University of Chicago Press.

Mitchem, Jeffrey M. 1991. Eleven Months of Mississippian Archeology at Parkin, 1990–1991. Paper presented at forty-eighth annual meeting, Southeastern Archaeological Conference, Jackson, Miss.

Mithun, Marianne. 1979. Iroquoian. In *The Languages of Native America: Historical and Comparative Assessment*, ed. Lyle Campbell and Marianne Mithun, pp. 133–212. Austin: University of Texas Press.

Mochon, Marion Johnson. 1972. Language, History and Prehistory: Mississippian Lexico-Reconstruction. *American Antiquity* 37:478–503.

Moll, H. 1711. *Florida Called by ye French Louisana &c*. Map in the Louisiana Collection, Tulane University.

Montler, Timothy R., and Heather K. Hardy. 1990. The Phonology of Alabama Agent Agreement. *Word* 41:257–76.

Mooney, James. 1886 [1982]. The Sacred Formulas of the Cherokees. *Seventh Annual Report of the Bureau of American Ethnology*. Washington, D.C. Reprint, Nashville: Elder Publishers.

Mooney, Timothy. 1991. Many Choctaw Standing, an Inquiry into Cultural Compromise and Cultural Survival Reflected in Seven Choctaw Sites in East-Central Mississippi. Paper presented to the Department of Anthropology, University of North Carolina at Chapel Hill.

Moore, Clarence B. 1911. Some Aboriginal Sites on the Mississippi River. *Journal of the Academy of Natural Sciences of Philadelphia* 14:364–480.

Morse, Dan F. 1990. The Nodena Phase. In *Towns and Temples Along the Mississippi*, ed. David H. Dye and Cheryl A. Cox, pp. 69–97. Tuscaloosa: University of Alabama Press.

———. 1991. On the Possible Origin of the Quapaws in Northeast Arkansas. In *Arkansas Before the Americans*, ed. Hester A. Davis, pp. 40–54. Arkansas Archeological Survey Research Series no. 40.

Morse, Dan F., and Phyllis A. Morse. 1983. *Archaeology of the Central Mississippi Valley*. New York: Academic Press.

———. 1990. The Spanish Exploration of Arkansas. In *Columbian Consequences*. Vol. 2: *Archaeological and Historical Perspectives on the Spanish Borderlands East*, ed. David H. Thomas, pp. 197–210. Washington, D.C.: Smithsonian Institution Press.

Morse, Phyllis. 1990. The Parkin Site and the Parkin Phase. In *Towns and*

Temples Along the Mississippi, ed. David H. Dye and Cheryl A. Cox, pp. 118–34. Tuscaloosa: University of Alabama Press.

Moulton, Gary E. 1985. *The Papers of Chief John Ross*. 2 vols. Norman: University of Oklahoma Press.

Mühlhäusler, Peter. 1986. *Pidgin and Creole Linguistics*. Oxford: Basil Blackwell.

Munro, Pamela. 1985a. Chicasaw Accent and Verb Grades. In *Studia linguistica diachronica et synchronica: Werner Winter sexagenario ann MCMLXXXIII*, ed. U. Pieper and G. Stickel, pp. 581–91. Amsterdam: Mouton de Gruyter.

—————. 1985b. Proto-Muskogean LI and *li* deletion. Paper presented at the Conference on American Indian Languages, American Anthropological Association, Washington, D.C.

—————. 1987a. Introduction: Muskogean Studies at UCLA. In *Muskogean Linguistics*, ed. Pamela Munro, pp. 1–6. UCLA Occasional Papers in Linguistics 6. Los Angeles: UCLA Linguistics Department.

—————. 1987b. The Muskogean II Prefixes and Their Implications for Classification. Paper presented at the Kentucky Foreign Language Conference, Lexington.

—————. 1987c. Some Morphological Differences Between Chickasaw and Choctaw. In *Muskogean Linguistics*, ed. Pamela Munro, pp. 119–33. UCLA Occasional Papers in Linguistics 6. Los Angeles: UCLA Linguistics Department.

Munro, Pamela, G. Broadwell, D. Cline, A. Coh, E. Drechsel, H. Hardy, G. Kimball, and J. Martin. 1990. Muskogean Cognate Sets. Unpublished manuscript.

Munro, Pamela, and Lynn Gordon. 1982. Syntactic Relations in Western Muskogean: A Typological Perspective. *Language* 58:81–115.

Nicklas, T. Dale. 1974. *The Elements of Choctaw*. Ph.D. dissertation, University of Michigan. Ann Arbor: University Microfilms.

—————. 1979a. *Reference Grammar of the Choctaw Language*. Durant, Okla.: Choctaw Bilingual Education Program.

—————. 1979b. Sioan and Muskogean. In *Papers of the 1978 Mid-America Linguistics Conference*, ed. R. Cooley et al., pp. 44–58. Norman: Departments of Anthropology and Communication, University of Oklahoma.

—————. 1991. The Pronominal Inflection of the Biloxi Verb. In *1990 Mid-America Linguistics Conference Papers*, ed. Frances Ingemann, pp. 44–58. Lawrence: Department of Linguistics, University of Kansas.

Oré, Luís Gerónimo de. 1936. *The Martyrs of Florida (1513–1616)*. New York: Joseph F. Wagner.

Pareja, Francisco. 1612. *Catechismo y Breve Exposicion de la Doctrina Christiana Muy Util y Necessaria, Asi para los Españoles, como para los Naturales en Lengua Castellana y Timuquana.* Mexico: Imprenta de la Viuda de Pedro Balli.

————. 1627. *Cathecismo y Examen para los Qve Comvlgan, en Lengua Castellana y Timuquana.* Mexico: Imprenta de Juan Ruyz.

Pareto, Vilfredo. 1980. *Compendium of General Sociology.* Minneapolis: University of Minnesota Press.

Parmalee, Paul W. 1966. Animal Remains from the Banks Site. In *The Banks Village Site, Crittenden County, Arkansas,* ed. Gregory Perino, pp. 142–45. Missouri Archaeological Society, Memoir 4, Columbia.

Penman, John T. 1980. Archaeological Survey in Mississippi, 1974–1975. Mississippi Department of Archives and History Archaeological Reports, no. 2.

Perdue, Theda. 1982. Traditionalism in the Cherokee Nation: Resistance to the Constitution of 1827. *Georgia Historical Quarterly* 66:159–70.

————. 1983. *Cherokee Editor: The Writings of Elias Boudinot.* Knoxville: University of Tennessee Press.

Perino, Gregory, ed., 1966. *The Banks Village Site, Crittenden County, Arkansas.* Missouri Archaeological Society, Memoir 4. Columbia.

Phillips, Philip. 1970. *Archaeological Survey on the Lower Yazoo Basin, Mississippi, 1949–1955.* Papers of the Peabody Museum of Archaeology and Ethnology 60. Cambridge: Harvard University Press.

Phillips, Philip, James A. Ford, and James B. Griffin. 1951. *Archaeological Survey in the Lower Mississippi Alluvial Valley, 1940–1947.* Papers of the Peabody Museum of Archaeology and Ethnology 25. Cambridge: Harvard University Press.

Price, Barbara J. 1984. Competition, Productive Intensification, and Ranked Society: Speculations from Evolutionary Theory. In *Warfare, Culture, and Environment,* ed. R. Brian Ferguson, pp. 209–40. New York: Academic Press.

Price, James A., and James B. Griffin. 1979. *The Snodgrass Site of the Power Phase of Southeast Missouri.* Anthropological Papers No. 66. Museum of Anthropology, University of Michigan, Ann Arbor.

Price, James A., and Gregory L. Fox. 1993. Recent Investigations at Towosahgy State Historic Site. *Missouri Archaeologist* 51:1–71.

Pueyo, Juan de. 1695. Visitation of Guale and Mocama. Trans. John H. Hann. In Visitations and Revolts. *Florida Archaeology* 7:220–48.

Pulte, Williams. 1975a. Outline of Cherokee Grammar. In *Cherokee-English Dictionary,* ed. William Pulte, pp. 534–50. Tahlequah: Cherokee Nation of Oklahoma.

————. 1975b. The Position of Chickasaw in Western Muskogean. In *Studies in Southeastern Indian Languages,* ed. James M. Crawford, pp. 251–56. Athens: University of Georgia Press.

Rangel, Rodrigo. 1922. Narrative of de Soto's Expedition Based on the Diary of Rodrigo Rangel His Private Secretary. In *Narratives of the Career of Hernando de Soto in the Conquest of Florida,* ed. Edward G. Bourne, trans. Buckingham Smith, 2:41–150. New York: A. S. Barnes.

Rankin, Robert L. 1975. Dhegiha Siouan, Algonkian, and the Languages of the Southeast. Paper presented at the summer meeting of the Linguistics Society of America, Tampa.

————. 1977. From Verb to Auxiliary to Noun Classifier and Definite Article: Grammaticalization of the Siouan Verbs "Sit," "Stand," "Lie." In *Proceedings of the 1976 Mid-America Linguistics Conference,* ed. R. L. Brown et al., pp. 273–83. Minneapolis: University of Minnesota Press.

————. 1978. Some Unpublicized Areal Features of the Southeast. Paper presented at the Mid-America Linguistics Conference, Norman, Oklahoma.

————. 1980. Some Unpublicized Areal Features of the Southeast. *International Journal of American Linguistics* 46:44–45.

————. 1987a. Fricative *Ablaut* in Choctaw and Siouan. Paper presented at the Kentucky Foreign Language Conference, Lexington.

————. 1987b. Ponca, Biloxi and Hidatsa Glottal Stop and Quapaw Gemination as Historically Related Accentual Phenomena. In *1987 Mid-America Linguistics Conference Papers,* ed. Michael M. T. Henderson, pp. 252–62. Lawrence: Department of Linguistics, University of Kansas.

————. 1988a. Language Affiliations of Some de Soto Place Names in Arkansas. Paper presented at the "De Soto in Arkansas" Symposium, University of Arkansas Museum, Fayetteville.

————. 1988b. Ponca, Biloxi and Hidatsa Glottal Stop and Quapaw Gemination as Historically Related Accentual Phenomena. In *1987 Mid-America Linguistics Conference Papers,* ed. Michael M. T. Henderson, pp. 252–62. Lawrence: Department of Linguistics, University of Kansas.

————. 1988c. Quapaw: Genetic and Areal Affiliations. In *In Honor of Mary Haas: From the Haas Festival Conference on Native American Linguistics,* ed. William Shipley, pp. 629–50. Berlin: Mouton de Gruyter.

————. 1992. On Siouan Chronology. Paper presented at the Siouan and Caddoan Linguistics Conference, Columbia, Missouri.

Rebolledo, Diego de. 1657 [1986]. Translation of Governor Rebolledo's 1657 Visitation of Three Florida Provinces and Related Documents. Trans. John H. Hann. *Florida Archaeology* 2:81–146.

Renfrew, Colin, and John F. Cherry, eds. 1986. *Peer Polity Interaction and Socio-Political Change.* Cambridge: Cambridge University Press.

Romans, Bernard. 1962. *A Concise Natural History of East and West Florida.* Facsimile reproduction of the 1775 edition. Gainesville: University of Florida Press.

Ruiz de Salazar Vallecilla, Benito. 1650. Order to Antonio de Argüelles, St. Augustine, July 11, 1650. Trans. Eugene Lyon. Archivo General de las Indias, Santo Domingo 23, Stetson Collection.

Sabo, George, III. 1992. *Paths of Our Children.* Arkansas Archeological Survey Popular Series, no. 3.

Sahagun, Fray Bernardino de. 1979. *General History of the Things of New Spain.* Trans. Arthur J. O. Anderson and Charles E. Dibble. Monographs of the School of American Research, no. 14, pt. 9. Santa Fe, New Mexico.

Scarry, John F. 1990. The Rise, Transformation, and Fall of Apalachee. In *Lamar Archaeology: Mississippian Chiefdoms in the Deep South,* ed. Mark Williams and Gary Shapiro, pp. 175–86. Tuscaloosa: University of Alabama Press.

Schoolcraft, Henry R. 1857. *Information Respecting the History, Condition and Prospects of the Indian Tribes of the United States.* Part 5. Philadelphia: J. B. Lippincott.

Siebert, Frank T., Jr. 1945. Linguistic Classification of Catawba: Parts I–II. *International Journal of the Sociology of Language* 11:100–104, 211–18.

Silverstein, Michael. 1973. Dynamics of Recent Linguistic Contact. Unpublished manuscript in author's files.

Smith, Bruce D., ed. 1978. *Mississippian Settlement Patterns.* New York: Academic Press.

———. 1984. Mississippian Expansion: Tracing the Historical Development of an Explanatory Model. *Southeastern Archaeology* 3:13–32.

———. 1985. Mississippian Patterns of Subsistence and Settlement. In *Alabama and the Borderlands. From Prehistory to Statehood,* ed. R. Reid Badger and Lawrence A. Clayton, pp. 64–79. University: University of Alabama Press.

———. 1990. *The Mississippian Emergence.* Washington, D.C.: Smithsonian Institution Press.

Smith, Gerald P. 1990. The Walls Phase and Its Neighbors. In *Towns and Temples Along the Mississippi,* ed. David H. Dye and Cheryl A. Cox, pp. 135–69. Tuscaloosa: University of Alabama Press.

Smith, Marvin T. 1987. *Archaeology of Aboriginal Culture Change in the Interior Southeast.* Gainesville: University Presses of Florida and Florida State Museum.

Solís de Merás, Gonzalo. 1923. Pedro Menéndez de Avilés, Adelantado, Governor and Captain-General of Florida: Memorial by Gonzalo Solís de Merás. Trans. Jeannette Thurber Connor. Deland: Florida State Historical Society.

Speck, Frank G. 1907. Some Comparative Traits of the Muskogean Languages. *American Anthropologist* 9:470–83.

———. 1909. *Ethnology of the Yuchi Indians.* Anthropological Publications of the University of Pennsylvania Museum, no. 1, pt. 1. Philadelphia: University of Pennsylvania Press.

Steinen, Karl T. 1992. Ambushes, Raids and Palisades: Mississippian Warfare in the Interior Southeast. *Southeastern Archaeology* 11:132–39.

Stowe, Noel R., Richard S. Fuller, Amy Snow, and Jennie Trimble. 1982. A Preliminary Report on the Pine Log Creek Site 1Ba462. University of South Alabama Archaeological Research Laboratory, Mobile.

Sturtevant, William C. 1962. Spanish-Indian Relations in Southeastern North America. *Ethnohistory* 9:41–94.

Swadesh, Morris. 1946a. Chitimacha. In *Linguistic Structures of Native America,* ed. Harry Hoijer, pp. 312–66. New York: Viking Fund.

———. 1946b. Phonological Formulas for Atakapa-Chitimacha. *International Journal of American Linguistics* 12:113–32.

Swanton, John R. 1911. *Indian Tribes of the Lower Mississippi Valley and Adjacent Coast of the Gulf of Mexico.* Bureau of American Ethnology Bulletin 43. Washington, D.C.

———. 1919. *A Structural and Lexical Comparison of the Tunica, Chitimacha, and Atakapa Languages.* Bureau of American Ethnology Bulletin 68. Washington, D.C.

———. 1922. *Early History of the Creek Indians and Their Neighbors.* Washington, D.C.

———. 1924. The Muskhogean Connection of the Natchez Language. *International Journal of American Linguistics* 3:46–75.

———. 1928. Sun Worship in the Southeast. *American Anthropologist,* n.s., 30:206–13.

———. 1929a. *Myths and Tales of the Southeastern Indians.* Bureau of American Ethnology Bulletin 88. Washington, D.C.

———. 1929b. A Sketch of the Atakapa Language. *International Journal of American Linguistics* 5:121–49.

———. 1932. Ethnological Value of the de Soto Narratives. *American Anthropologist* 34:570–90.

———. 1939. *Final Report of the United States de Soto Commission.* House of Representatives Document no. 71. Washington, D.C.: Government Printing Office.

———. 1942. *Source Material in the History and Ethnology of the Caddo Indians.* Bureau of American Ethnology Bulletin 132. Washington, D.C.

———. 1991. A Grammatical Sketch of the Natchez Language. Manuscript edited and annotated by T. Dale Nicklas.

Tesar, Louis D. 1974. Archaeological Assessment of the Tallahala Reservoir Area, Jasper County, Mississippi. Report submitted to the Department of the Interior, National Park Service. Department of Anthropology, Mississippi State University, Starkville.

Thomason, Sarah Grey. 1983. Chinook Jargon in Areal and Historic Context. *Language* 59:820–70.

Thomason, Sarah Grey, and Terrence Kaufman. 1988. *Language Contact, Creolization, and Genetic Linguistics*. Berkeley: University of California Press.

Traveler Bird. 1971. *Tell Them They Lie: The Sequoyah Myth*. Los Angeles: Westernlore Publishers.

Tregle, Joseph G., Jr., ed. 1975. *The History of Louisiana: Translated from the French of M. Le Page du Pratz*. Baton Rouge: Louisiana State University Press.

Turner, Victor. 1970. *The Forest of Symbols*. Ithaca: Cornell University Press.

Tylor, Edward B. 1913. *Primitive Culture*. London: J. Murray.

Ulrich, Charles H. 1986. Choctaw Morphophonology. Ph.D. dissertation, University of California, Los Angeles.

———. 1993. The Glottal Stop in Western Muskogean. *International Journal of American Linguistics* 59.

Varner, John, and Jeannette Varner. 1951. *The Florida of the Inca*. Austin: University of Texas Press.

Vayda, Andrew P. 1956. *Maori Warfare*. Ph.D. dissertation, Columbia University. Ann Arbor: University Microfilms.

Voorhis, Paul. n.d. Catawba. Unpublished manuscript in author's files.

Voss, Jerome A., and John H. Blitz. 1988. Archaeological Investigations in the Choctaw Homeland. *American Antiquity* 53:125–45.

Wagner, Gunter. 1931. *Yuchi Tales*. Publications of the American Ethnological Society 13. Washington, D.C.

———. 1934. Yuchi. In *Handbook of American Indian Languages*, vol. 3, ed. Franz Boas, pp. 293–384. New York: Columbia University Press.

Walker, Willard. 1969. Notes on Native Writing Systems and the Design of Native Literacy Programs. *Anthropological Linguistics* 11:148–66.

———. 1975. Cherokee. In *Studies in Southeastern Indian Languages*, ed. James M. Crawford, pp. 189–236. Athens: University of Georgia Press.

Wallace, Anthony F. C. 1956. Revitalization Movements. *American Anthropologist* 58:264–81.

Walthall, John A. 1980. *Prehistoric Indians of the Southeast*. University: University of Alabama Press.

Weinstein, Richard A. 1985. Some New Thoughts on the de Soto Expedition Through Western Mississippi. *Mississippi Archaeology* 20:2–14.

————. 1992. The de Soto Expedition and Its Route Through Western Mississippi. Unpublished manuscript in author's files.

Williams, Mark, and Gary Shapiro. 1990. Introduction. In *Lamar Archaeology: Mississippian Chiefdoms in the Deep South,* ed. M. Williams and G. Shapiro, pp. 3–9. University: University of Alabama Press.

Williams, J. Raymond. 1964. A Study of Fortified Indian Villages in Southeastern Missouri. Master's thesis, University of Missouri, Columbia.

Williams, Samuel C. 1973. *Adair's History of the American Indians.* New York: Promontory Press.

Williams, Stephen. 1980. The Armorel Phase: A Very Late Complex in the Lower Mississippi Valley. *Southeastern Archaeological Conference Bulletin* 22:105–10.

Williams, Stephen, and Jeffrey P. Brain. 1983. *Excavations at the Lake George Site, Yazoo County, Mississippi, 1958–1960.* Papers of the Peabody Museum of Archaeology and Ethnology 74. Cambridge: Harvard University Press.

Willis, William S., Jr. 1980. Fusion and Separation: Archaeology and Ethnohistory in Southeastern North America. In *Theory and Practice: Essays Presented to Gene Weltfish,* ed. Stanley Diamond, pp. 97–123. The Hague: Mouton.

Woodward, Grace Steele. 1963. *The Cherokees.* Norman: University of Oklahoma Press.

Zubillaga, Felix, ed. 1946. *Monumenta Antiquae Floridae (1566–1572).* Monumenta Missionum Societatis Jesu, no. 3. Rome.

Contributors

KENNETH H. CARLETON is the tribal archaeologist for the Mississippi Band of Choctaw Indians. He received his M.A. in anthropology from the University of Georgia.

EMANUEL J. DRECHSEL is an associate professor of linguistics at the University of Hawai'i at Mānoa.

DAVID H. DYE is an associate professor of anthropology at Memphis State University. He has conducted archaeological and ethnographic fieldwork throughout the Mid-South and has recently turned his attention to the ethnohistory of the Mid-South in the sixteenth century. His particular interest is the contact between the Mississippian people of the central Mississippi Valley and the Hernando de Soto expedition.

JOHN H. HANN is the site historian at the San Luis Archaeological and Historic Site in Tallahassee, Florida.

MICHAEL P. HOFFMAN is a professor of anthropology at the University of Arkansas and anthropology curator at the University Museum. His research interests include Native Americans of the Mississippian and protohistoric periods in the Southeast.

GREG KEYES is currently pursuing his M.A. in anthropology at the University of Georgia with an emphasis in ethnohistory. His research focuses on the mythology of the southeastern Indians.

GEOFFREY KIMBALL is a visiting assistant professor of linguistics at Tulane University. He is the author of *Koasati Grammar* (1991).

PATRICIA B. KWACHKA is an associate professor of anthropology at the University of Alaska, Fairbanks, and the tribal linguist for the Mississippi Band of Choctaw Indians. Her research interests include language maintenance and language shift.

JACK MARTIN is a visiting assistant professor of linguistics and semiotics at Rice University. His research interests include the historical relationships of southeastern and Muskogean languages.

JOHN H. MOORE is a professor of anthropology at the University of Oklahoma. He is the author of *The Cheyenne Nation: A Social and Demographic History* (1987) and editor of *Political Economy of North American Indians* (1993). He has conducted extensive fieldwork with the Creek and Seminole Indians of Oklahoma.

T. DALE NICKLAS is a practicing attorney in Lawrence, Kansas, and a linguist. He received his Ph.D. in linguistics from the University of Michigan at Ann Arbor.

THEDA PERDUE, a professor of history at the University of Kentucky, is the author of *Slavery and the Evolution of Cherokee Society* (1979), *Native Carolinians* (1985), and *The Cherokee* (1988). She is the editor of *Nations Remembered: An Oral History of the Five Civilized Tribes* (1980) and *Cherokee Editor: The Writings of Elias Boudinot* (1983).